Risk Management
in Public Contracting

Elisabeth Wright, Ph.D., CPCM

Prepared for NIGP: The Institute for Public Procurement. All rights are conveyed to the NIGP upon completion of this book.

Risk Management *in* Public Contracting

Information in this book is accurate as of the time of publication and consistent with generally accepted public purchasing principles. However, as research and practice advance, standards may change. For this reason, it is recommended that readers evaluate the applicability of any recommendation in light of particular situations and changing standards.

National Institute of Governmental Purchasing, Inc. (NIGP)
151 Spring Street
Herndon, VA 20170
Phone: 703-736-8900; 800-367-6447
Fax: 703-736-9639 Email: education@nigp.org

This book is available at a special discount when ordered in bulk quantities. For information, contact NIGP at 800-367-6447. A complete catalog of titles is available on the NIGP website at www.nigp.org.

ISBN 978-1-932315-11-0

This book was set in Berkeley Oldstyle
Design & production by Vizuäl, Inc. - www.vizual.com.
Printed & bound by HBP.

Acknowledgements

The author wishes to acknowledge NIGP for its commitment toward advancing the theories and practices in procurement and contracting. Without their support this text would not have been possible.

Thanks and best,

Elisabeth Wright, Ph. D., CPCM
Program Manager
School of International Studies
U. S. Naval Postgraduate School
Monterey, CA

CONTENTS

Introduction

The management and administration of public sector contracts pose unique challenges. Billions of tax dollars are spent each year purchasing construction, supplies and services in support of public facilities. The particular features of public sector contracts and the special obligations that accompany any expenditure of public funds complicate the management of these efforts.

Risk is a critical consideration in the contracting and procurement process. A thoughtful and proactive approach toward risk, as it relates to specific procurement actions, contributes to the success of contract performance. Risk is directly related to the successful achievement of targeted goals and objectives. The procurement manager must ensure that the risks associated with each procurement action have been identified, assessed, and mitigated to the practicable maximum extent, while taking cost and other factors into consideration.

Risk does not exist in a vacuum, nor does it end at the time the contract is awarded. Risk management is an iterative process that continues through the pre-award and post-award phases of a contract. It is complicated by the dynamics of the internal and external operating environments. Given these dynamics, the risk management plan is a living document that must undergo constant review and adjustments necessary to meet the changing demands posed by the operating environment. Emphasis in this text will focus on developing a solid understanding of the complexities of risk management and recognizing the importance of planning, monitoring and proactive insight and oversight into risk areas related to the contract's stated performance outputs and outcomes.

Knowledge information can be grouped into three broad categories: what we know we know; what we know we don't know; and what we don't know that we don't know. This final category poses the most challenges. Further complicating risk management is the theory of bounded rationality (Simon, 1956). The bounded rationality theory suggests that the search for a solution will continue until a satisfactory solution is found. In other words, the best or perfect solution will not be sought once a solution that satisfies the situation is identified. This predisposition toward seeking limited solutions further complicates the risk management process.

Many solutions that present possible alternatives to manage and mitigate risk may appear attractive; however, a balance between affordability and practicability is a key consideration. Managers who deal with risk must also be cognizant of applicable laws, regulations and policies. The manager must exercise good judgment and apply critical thinking to the risk management decisions. Knowledge and the ability to apply reasoning and analytical skills to the examination of risk issues are critical components of successful risk management.

This book intends to provide a framework for examining risk management by focusing on the components of risk as they relate to contract management. It will provide the reader with a road map for framing and examining the key considerations regarding risk that must be explored throughout the acquisition cycle. It is recommended that participants in risk management examine other texts that deal with statistical probability, since quantitative techniques are useful in risk management.

The scope of this text is limited and, therefore, has been designed to provide an understanding of risk management and the functions and considerations related to risk that contribute to successful contract formation and administration. It provides a framework for examining risk and a suggested template that managers may find useful in their efforts to identify and manage contract-related risk. The practitioner is reminded that while the fundamentals of risk management transcend specific contract requirements, risk management itself must be unique to each contract in order to be effective. Adopting a single risk management plan to govern a group of contracts is not good practice because each contract has unique features and different goals and objectives. In other words, "one size does not fit all." The relationship between the contracting parties, the type of contract and the stated outputs and outcomes of the contract all influence the risk management plan. A good risk management plan will contribute to successful requirements definition, solicitation drafting, source selection outcomes and contract administration. The ultimate goal is to anticipate risk areas and adopt a risk mitigation plan that will control the risk. A well-developed and thoughtful risk management plan will enable the procurement manager to be proactive rather than reactive as problems arise during the procurement process.

These materials have been addressed from a global perspective, i.e., unique statutes and/or regulations may be mentioned. However, the material transcends state- or national-level interests by reviewing risk management best practices that apply regardless of specific jurisdictional laws and regulations that may govern.

Non-procurement members of the contract management team might benefit from particular topics of interest. For example, the discussion of risk as it relates to scheduling will be useful for those managers charged with estimating and defining required delivery/performance dates. Additionally, performance monitoring personnel will find the discussion of root cause analysis and other techniques for identifying and mitigating risk beneficial.

Chapter 1

Defining Risk within the Procurement Cycle

R isk takes many shapes and forms. Webster's dictionary defines risk as "the chance of injury, damage or loss." Within the context of procurement, risk will be examined by defining it as it relates to the procurement discipline. Risk can be further defined as the probability of some occurrence (e.g., a failure) and the consequences and impact of the occurrence. Oftentimes, risk cannot be avoided. Attempting to avoid risk can result in an unacceptable drain on resources. Rather, risk management should focus on the development and use of a well-designed plan, which identifies sources of risk, likelihood of risk occurrence, consequences of realized risk, and steps that can be taken to proactively manage the risk.

Effective risk management depends on established, meaningful metrics with which to measure progress toward successful contract completion, given the dynamics of the internal and external operating environment. **If you do not have metrics, you are not managing.**

During the procurement process, many things can go wrong. The challenge lies in having the foresight to reasonably identify what can go wrong and implement risk management techniques. Further complicating this procedure are the dynamics that cloud attempts to assess potential impacts and the causes of such impacts. Cause and effect must be linked to affect a successful risk management program. Treating the symptoms rather than the cause does not foster systemic improvement.

Risk management requires planning for risk, assessing risk types and areas, and developing risk management options. Once these initial steps have been taken, the procurement manager must continue to monitor risks to identify changes within the internal and external environments that may impact the initial risk assessment. Inherent in risk planning is the need to develop and document a well-organized and comprehensive strategy that includes the methods that will be used to assess, track and measure risk.

While some organizations assign the risk management function to a member of the management team, it or some subset of the elements of the risk management function can also be the responsibility of the procurement manager. The decision to assign risk management responsibilities will depend on the size, scope and complexity of the procurement, available expertise and the organizational structure.

Risk Planning. Too often risk management plans are implemented but are not used, refined or updated as events occur. Proper planning requires the development of a risk plan that is dynamic rather than static. Those responsible for risk management must ensure that the adopted plan is used and amended so that it contains the most current information. A common technique for indicating updates is through the use of revision numbers. This method preserves the language of the initial plan and updates relevant parts of the plan through the addition of sequential revisions.

Risk Assessment. Assessment of the risk requires the procurement manager to identify and analyze procurement and related risks so that opportunities can be identified to manage or avoid the risk. Risk assessment should also include a "ranking order" of the risk areas that have been identified and a thorough examination of the interrelationships that may exist among the risk areas.

Risk Handling. Risk handling examines the options that are available to manage or control the risk. Risk handling options should include a wide spectrum of opportunities, recognizing that options, which are not obvious or may be considered extreme, may actually prove to be good solutions. Risk handling is an important component of the risk management plan because it identifies the options, criteria for enactment of an option and responsibilities for taking action. The range of risk can be broad, necessitating shared risk management responsibilities among various departments within an organization.

Risk Monitoring. Monitoring risk requires the risk manager(s) to stay current regarding the dynamics of the internal and external environments so that events that may trigger risk are quickly identified. Effective risk monitoring is necessary to successfully manage risk because it is unlikely that risk will continue to exist in a steady state.

Risk Documentation. Documentation is also a key component of the risk management process. The quality of the documentation is important because formal documentation provides the framework and the "history" of the risk issues. Corporate memory is not sufficient for managing risk. Rather, accurate, complete and current documentation that clearly delineates all aspects of the risk management plan and processes related to the procurement must be available. Such documentation provides the baseline document as well as the updated documents that record the events surrounding the procurement action and keep the procurement team current on events that have transpired. These records also serve as the basis for documenting risk-related decisions that may be examined at a later date. Risk management plans should be a part of the official contract file.

Risk management is the responsibility of both parties to the contract. During the pre-solicitation phase, risk assessment should be a key consideration in a variety of decisions, ranging from contract type to the nature of terms and conditions that will apply to the contract. During this period, there is significant opportunity for dialogue between suppliers and procurement staff. This dialogue can make a significant contribution to the development of a well-constructed acquisition strategy. During the solicitation and source selection phases, risk continues to be of interest to both parties. Suppliers are assessing the impact of proposed terms and conditions vis-à-vis their pricing strategy. Public agency evaluators are evaluating proposals to determine the risk associated with, among other things, technical approach, capabilities, and prices submitted by various proponents. During the contract administration phase, both parties should continually monitor contract performance as it relates to the degree of risk each assumed at the time of contract formation.

Within the public agency team, risk management responsibilities must be specific and precise. The delegation of risk management responsibilities will differ in centralized and decentralized organizations. Nonetheless, responsibilities must be clear and unambiguous. Additionally, care must be taken to avoid delegation of responsibilities that overlap among individuals, as this will cause confusion and problems with accountability. Delegation of risk management responsibility should be made in writing and should detail the specific areas of responsibility assigned to each individual. Responsibility for reporting and documenting findings and conclusions related to specific risk management assignments should be included as a part of this delegation.

If the risk management team approach rather than single delegation is used, it is very important to identify the "owner" of the risk management plan. Doing so will avoid uncoordinated, uncontrolled and unapproved changes to the plan. Once the owner has been identified, proposed and approved changes are forwarded to the risk management coordinator (owner) who controls all changes to the official risk management plan. If and when the owner changes, all appropriate personnel should be notified so that uninterrupted coordination continues.

Public Agency View of Risk

The public agency, as the buyer, must view risk with a cautious eye. A significant expenditure of public funds occurs in the contracting process, and the public agency has a fiduciary duty of care and trust in obligating and expending those funds. Given this somber responsibility, public agency procurement staff is charged with examining risk from both perspectives—the buyer and the seller. The appropriate balance of risk, given the circumstance of each procurement, plays a vital role in the public agency decision-making process. The appropriate balance of risk between the parties aims to avoid the unnecessary expenditure of public funds by protecting the supplier and the public agency from undue risk. In other words, the focus should not shift undue risk onto the supplier

At one end of the continuum, risk avoidance may be considered a viable alternative to managing risk. However, on a practical level, risk avoidance can be expensive. As the continuum moves to the right, the risk manager examines possibilities that are more affordable, such as risk sharing. At the other extreme is risk assumption. Risk assumption means that the risk manager is willing to assume the risk associated with some particular event. The decision that the risk manager makes regarding the risk strategy will differ for each procurement action. Consider the manager who desires a delivery date that is unreasonable from an industry perspective. The risk associated with delivery can be handled in several ways. The public agency can avoid the risk by changing the delivery date; or perhaps the public agency can build an incentive into the contract, which effectively shares the risk of delivery between the contracting parties. Alternatively, the public agency can assume the risk by entertaining higher priced bids that meet the delivery date.

Acquisition Management and Risk

We can examine contract management and risk by segregating contract management into discrete areas:

Pre-Award. The pre-award phase includes all actions that take place prior to the execution of the contract. The assessment of risk continues throughout all segments of this phase, and risk identification and assessment can change as more information is gathered through the phase. Additionally, various risk areas can surface and recede like tides as the environment that makes risk a possibility changes. The importance of risk management in the pre-award phase cannot be over-emphasized. All intended actions and their possible consequences must be carefully considered in a risk management plan so that the risk associated with each can be carefully assessed and examined for possible mitigation techniques.

Market Research. The market surveillance and market research actions of the contract manager will provide much valuable information about risk as it relates to the instant procurement. Market surveillance provides an understanding of the industry and the market forces that influence the industry. Market research is the gathering of more specific information, i.e., information related to a particular source or number of sources within an industry. Market surveillance is an ongoing process that allows the contract manager to continually gather general information about trends in a particular industry. Together, market surveillance and market research information provide the contract manager with important information with which to assess areas of possible risk and the factors that contribute to or control risk.

> *Question for Consideration: Identify some techniques for conducting market surveillance and market research. What types of risk might you identify and/or possibly mitigate by conducting market research?*

Request for Proposal/Bid. During the preparation of the solicitation and its formal release, careful assessment of the implications of proposed terms and conditions is necessary. If not carefully considered, the terms and conditions contained within the solicitation may actually be a deterrent to a possible supplier submitting a bid. The market research information should be used to provide reasonable terms and conditions, including contract type, within the solicitation that will not place undue or unnecessary risk on a viable supplier. Consider the inclusion of required delivery dates. If the public agency requires an unrealistic delivery date that is in conflict with market research information, potential suppliers may decide to "no bid" the work. Alternatively, suppliers may build in contingency costs to offset possible additional costs, which could make the price unaffordable, e.g., overtime, express shipping costs, etc. Good risk assessment recognizes the consequences of setting an unrealistic delivery date and prepares the contract manager to deal with the issue in a timely manner. It may be that the contract management team needs to seek alternatives to an unreasonable delivery date.

Evaluation. The evaluation process must consider the risks inherent in a supplier's proposal. The evaluation criteria should include risk as an important part of the evaluation process. Risk may be associated with many aspects of performance, e.g., labor skills, mix and quantity of personnel. Management approach may also be a risk area. Proponents whose proposals fail to indicate the level of management interest and commitment toward contract success warrant a higher risk rating than those who clearly define management's commitment.

Risk can be categorized by numeric, alpha, or color. For example, the evaluation plan may recognize three ranges of risk: high, medium or low. Each range should include a narrative description of what constitutes a risk falling within that range, e.g., High Risk: A proposal is considered high risk if it includes unproven technical solutions or an unrealistic production schedule.

In many public sector environments, the evaluation of risk does not need to be specifically called for because it is considered a part of the routine evaluation process. In Federal Government procurement, regulatory language states that the evaluation of risk is inherent in the proposal evaluation process.

Matrix- Risk Assessment for Liability

		Severity			
		Catastrophic	Major	Moderate	Minor
PROBABILITY	Frequent	3	3	2	1
	Occasional	3	2	1	1
	Uncommon	3	2	1	1
	Remote	3	2	1	1

How the Matrix Works:

When you pair a *severity category* with a probability category you will get a ranked matrix score:

- highest risk = 3 e.g. construction work in a public area
- intermediate risk = 2 e.g. certified diver recovering golf balls from a water hazard
- lowest risk = 1 e.g. consultant reviewing materials and reporting

List Key Factors for the severity categories are: *(To be completed during discussions relevant to the specific situation.)*

In order to assign a *probability rating*, it is important to know if there have been any past experiences of issues/problems.

- Frequent – likely to occur immediately or within a short period of time
- Occasional – probably may occur in time
- Uncommon – possible to occur in time
- Remote – highly unlikely

Source Selection. The source selection process requires that the evaluation plan's stated procedures regarding the assessment of risk be followed. Each proposal must be evaluated and reviewed with a thorough examination of the risks associated with the proposal. The use of evaluators who are recognized as subject-matter experts is a key ingredient of successful risk assessment in source selection. The risk associated with all offers can be categorized into two groupings.

- *Proposal Risk.* Proposal risk is the term used to describe the aspects of the proposal itself that pose some degree of risk. Proposal risk may be associated with the proponent's proposed technical approach or proposed solutions for meeting stated requirements. Proposal risk assessment can require some degree of subjectivity, and the informed judgments and opinions of subject-matter experts who conduct such evaluations will strengthen the quality of risk assessment at this juncture. Alternatively, proposal risk assessment can be based upon some objective measurable data, such as technical information found during market research that is counter to a proposal.

- *Performance Risk.* Performance risk examines the risk of success of performance given the capabilities of the proponent. For example, performance risk may be considered low for a particular proponent who demonstrates a strong record of success in accomplishing the same or similar types of work. If, however, a proponent has little or no experience (or perhaps prior failures), performance risk may be considered high.

Post-Award. Once the contract has been awarded, the continued evaluation and assessment of risk is necessary to ensure contract success. The degree of monitoring and surveillance of risk areas will vary depending upon the credentials, past performance and experience of the selected proponent. Notwithstanding the selection of a high quality proponent with a proven track record, some degree of monitoring and surveillance should continue to ensure that risk remains "on the radar scope." Failure to do so can force the contract manager to make decisions from a reactive position. In scenarios, which are considered low risk, the ongoing monitoring and surveillance can be of a routine nature. The objective is to ensure that low-risk items remain low risk.

Areas/Types of Risk

R isk can be broadly grouped into four areas: technical, schedule, cost/price and other. Within each of these areas, specific types of risk can exist. Note that none exist in a vacuum, i.e. they can be interrelated.

Technical Risk. Technical risk recognizes that some degree of risk may be associated with the technical aspects of a requirement or a proposal. The language of the specification or work statement can drive that risk, or it can be a function of the contractor's technical proposal. Technical risk assesses the degree of confidence the evaluators have regarding successful technical performance of the work. As stated earlier, identification and assessment of technical risk can require subjectivity; thus, evaluators should be knowledgeable in the technical discipline.

Schedule Risk. Schedule risk defines the degree of risk that is associated with meeting the schedule. If the schedule is aggressive, the level of risk may be high, and various risk mitigation factors may be identified. If the public agency mandates the schedule or delivery date, the public agency staff must recognize early in the acquisition phase the consequences of setting such a schedule. If the supplier proposes an unrealistic schedule, the technical approach and price to evaluate any mitigating factors that may exist within those two areas that would make an otherwise unrealistic schedule realistic must be examined. Market surveillance and research form the foundation for risk assessments regarding schedule.

Cost/Price. There can be a level of risk associated with the cost/price proposed by a supplier. Cost risk assessment concerns itself with an examination of the elements of cost included within the contract price to determine whether the costs accurately represent those that could be incurred during contract performance. Price risk, however, concerns itself with the reasonableness of the proposed price. If cost visibility exists, the contract manager should examine the elements of costs, particularly cost drivers. Price is always evaluated regardless of whether or not cost is evaluated. If costs are not included that should reasonably have been included, a careful examination of the technical proposal should be conducted to ascertain the reason for the lack of certain proposed costs. Failure of a proponent to include costs necessary for successful completion of the contract poses a risk to successful performance of the work. The evaluation of the price from a risk perspective helps to ascertain the reasonableness of the price to perform the work as proposed. A price that is unreasonably low may jeopardize successful contract performance, thus posing a risk.

Other. Other types of risk can exist in contractual arrangements. These include supportability of a system over its useful service life, fluctuations in currency and political unrest in a particular region or country.

Figure 2 demonstrates risk assessment. This example includes supportability as an area of possible risk.

RATING	TECHNICAL	SCHEDULE	COST	SUPPORTABILITY
Low	Previously demonstrated technology Requires integration and testing Manageable within PM's discretion	Plans and forecasts indicate successful accomplishment of milestone within 10% of planned schedule	Actuals plus forecasts indicate completion within < 10% growth of anticipated costs	Likely to meet supportability requirements
Moderate	Prototype technology demonstrated Design iterations and testing required Potential serious impacts, but manageable within current requirements	Plans and forecasts indicate a potential of >10%; but <20% additional schedule growth may be required	Actuals plus forecasts indicate >10% but ≤ 20% growth of anticipated costs Manageable within current management reserves	Possible support constraints or deficiencies Sustainment cost constraints
High	Concept and/or technology not demonstrated Current analysis not conclusive Potential major impact that would require program restructure and/or revision of requirements	Plans and forecasts indicate a potential of >20%; additional schedule resources may be required	Actuals plus forecasts indicate >20% growth of anticipated costs Resources required exceed management reserves	Potential major impact on supportability

Figure 2. Risk Matrix—Risk Level Definitions

What Do I Do Now?

Michael Shouldknow, Procurement Specialist for the Happy Hollow Long-Term Care & Retirement Home, issued a competitive sealed proposal to hire a consultant to undertake a comprehensive review of the Home's staffing structure, staffing levels and compensation structure.

Happy Hollow management was proud of their facility and wanted only the best for their residences. They were adamant that Michael make this crystal clear in the document he issued and make sure that only well qualified companies responded. Michael wrote the document with this in mind but found it challenging to develop requirements and criteria that would ensure the required responses. Ultimately, the document was issued and the Specifications stated that all proponents must submit the following information in their proposal response:

1) Proof of insurance as follows:

   a. General Liability in the amount of $2,000,000,

   b. Vehicles (owned and non-owned) in the amount of $1,000,000, and,

   c. Errors and Omissions in the amount of $2,000,000;

2) Proof of Workers Compensation coverage; and,

3) A minimum of three references from healthcare providers in the State.

During the bid period, representatives from two major consulting firms called Michael requesting clarification on these specific requirements and his expectations. They also stated that the levels of insurance required were not standard for their industry. Michael replied "Happy Hollow only wants the best for its residents and we aren't prepared to change the requirements".

When the bid period closed and responses were reviewed for compliance, Michael was appalled to find that not one of them met all of these requirements. He knew that since his document stated these were mandatory requirements, he would have to declare all of the responses invalid and re-issue. He had no idea how he was going to explain this to his manager, Hank Thinkfast, and the Home's CEO, Dr. Googleheim.

Questions:

   1) Identify the potential risks involved in this type of work.

   2) How could Michael have avoided the situation in which he now finds himself?

Summary

This chapter introduced the various components of the risk management process. Risk management must be conducted initially in the early phases of the acquisition process and must continue throughout the acquisition life cycle. The following points are critically important to successful risk management:

- Solid market surveillance and research;

- Development of levels of risk and the consequences of each risk, if realized;

- Coordinated efforts and reliance on subject-matter experts as part of risk management;

- Ongoing risk management through the use of surveillance and monitoring;

- Reliance on the supplier to utilize best practices, thus mitigating unnecessary risk;

- Management and updating of the risk management plan through the efforts of a central authority (an owner) to ensure control over the process; and

- Reliance on a risk management plan that is accurate, complete and current.

Chapter 2

Framework and Assessment

Effective risk management creates a framework for the performance of all related contractual and programmatic activities. Because risk is viewed through various lenses and many types and levels of risk exist, the contract manager faces challenging complexities. While poor planning and ineffective management are proven contributors to contractual problems, a lack of effective identification, assessment and management of risk can easily doom a contract and program to fail.

A Framework for Managing Risk

A well-defined output- and outcome-based process is an effective means of managing risk. Using this process, risks associated with both immediate results (outputs) and any long-term, overall, or residual results (outcome) can be more clearly defined and adequately assessed. The four-phase process model described below can be used to frame and categorize the risk phenomenon. It also forms the foundation for development of a risk mitigation plan. It is important to remember that the nature of risk and its dynamic relationship to the operating environment dictates ongoing assessment and monitoring. Furthermore, risk variations among contracts make a "cookbook" approach dangerous. Rather, the contract manager can adopt the four-phase process, recognizing that the types and levels of risk and the management of risk will vary from contract to contract.

The four-phase process model provides a structured methodology for framing the important risk considerations. It is a sequential model that relies on the process outputs from previous phases. The various risk mitigation techniques are applied to specific situations throughout the sequence of activities.

The value of teams is an effective means of populating the model. The team approach offers a valuable opportunity to view risk through the lens of the various functional disciplines. Early identification of risk sets the stage for a proactive, rather than a reactive, approach to problem solving. Furthermore, a verification and validation loop that traces key operational, programmatic and contractual elements to the risk model offers an effective means for examining the completeness and accuracy of the risk management plan. Figure 3 provides a risk analysis example. Note the use of descriptors for each level of risk and the magnitude of the impact or risk at each level.

F/A-18 Program Risk Analysis

What is the Likelihood the Risk Will Happen?		
Level		*Your Approach and Processes...*
1	Not Likely:	...Will effectively avoid or mitigate this risk based on standard practices
2	Low Likelihood:	...Have usually mitigated this type of risk with minimal oversight in similar cases
3	Likely:	...May mitigate this risk, but workarounds will be required
4	Highly Likely:	...Cannot mitigate this risk, but a different approach might
5	Near Certainty:	...Cannot mitigate this type of risk; no known processes or workarounds are available

(Likelihood axis label on left)

Risk matrix chart: Likelihood (vertical, 1–5) vs Consequences (horizontal, 1–5), with LOW, MEDIUM, and HIGH regions.

Given the Risk is Realized, What Would be the Magnitude of the Impact?			
Level	*Technical*	*Schedule*	*Cost*
1	Minimal or no impact	Minimal or no impact	Minimal or no impact
2	Minor perf shortfall, same approach retained	Additional activities required; able to meet key dates	Budget increase or unit production cost increase <1%
3	Mod perf shortfall, but workarounds available	Minor schedule slip; will miss need date	Budget increase or unit production cost increase <5%
4	Unacceptable but workarounds available	Program critical path affected	Budget increase or unit production cost increase <10%
5	Unacceptable; no alternatives exist	Cannot achieve key program milestone	Budget increase or unit production cost increase >10%

(Consequences axis label on left)

Figure 3. Risk Analysis Example.

Phase 1: Risk Identification

During Phase 1, types of risk are identified. Risk identification includes a brief description of the risk as well as the perceived cause(s) of the risk. Answers to the questions "who, what, when, where and why" provide important information in this early phase of risk management. The type of risks that are identified should be critical parameters of contract and program success. Technical, performance, schedule, contract type and cost are commonly recognized as risk areas that must be examined during the risk identification phase. Additionally, environmental, political, economic, financial and organizational states are possible sources of risk.

> *Question for Consideration: Can you identify risk factors that must be considered in the programs and contracts within your organization? How do you attempt to manage such risks?*

The identification of risk is an iterative process, i.e., initial risk identification must be reexamined and updated as the internal and external environment changes.

Phase 2: Risk Assessment

Phase 2 requires that an assessment be conducted to show the degree of risk that exists for each identified risk type. Although this assessment can be based upon various mathematical models, it is ultimately a subjective process because the mathematical models require input of initial data that is subjectively derived. Degrees of risk can be categorized using adjectival ratings, numerical ratings, or colors. A range of risk exists within each defined category. Categories must cover the risk continuum, i.e., degrees of risk ranging from high risk to low risk. The use of descriptors indicates the characteristics that must be present for a risk element to meet the conditions of a pre-defined risk level. Categories that lack descriptors are not useful because evaluators will be forced to categorize risk elements using their own descriptors. Figure 4 provides a generic example of degrees of risk and broad descriptors. From a practical perspective, "all things are not equal" within a risk category. In other words, there are sub-categories that are inherent in broad categorization of a risk element. This concept is easily understood by examining the numerical approach. Assignment of medium risk in Figure 4 offers a range of numerics ranging from four at the low end to seven at the high end. The descriptors that support the selection of a specific category provide the important differentiation necessary to evaluate, e.g., competing approaches. While two proposed approaches to achieving a technical solution might be considered medium risk, one might be considered a higher risk than the other.

The likelihood that an identified risk will occur is an important component of risk assessment. Figure 4 also provides an example of risk likelihood definitions. To characterize the likelihood of risk, a general question is posed.

Question: What is the likelihood that the risk will occur?

Not Likely: There is very little likelihood of a negative impact or outcome based upon standard practices and/or procedures. This is based upon factual information or previous experience (define to what extent, if any) that the assessment is subjective. This assessment assignment requires a well documented and understood approach to prevent or avoid the risk. Little, if any, oversight will be required at this risk level.

Low Likelihood: It is unlikely that the risk will occur. Some monitoring and surveillance will be required. Monitoring will help ensure that the risk does not shift to a higher level of probability.

Moderate Likelihood: The possibility exists that the risk will occur. Ongoing monitoring and surveillance is necessary. A risk mitigation plan must offer options for handling the risk event.

High Likelihood: It is likely that the risk will occur. Constant monitoring and surveillance at a high level must be in place. The risk mitigation plan must provide a contingency plan with which to address the risk.

Almost Certain: It is near certainty that the risk will occur. Risk mitigation techniques must address the risk and attempt to minimize its consequences to the extent practicable. Recognition of this type of risk requires analysis of options, given the seriousness of the consequences of realizing the risk.

Finally, managers should avoid "putting the cart before the horse," i.e., creating descriptors that have the unintended consequence of creating "a fit" for a particular risk element. Doing so will result in a distorted assessment of the types of risk in which the user can place no confidence.

Level of Risk	Adjectival	Numeric	Color	Description
High	High	8-10	Red	Significant risk to success of the intended outcome. Risk mitigation is unlikely or difficult and costly.
Medium	Medium	7-4	Yellow	Poses moderate risk to success of the intended outcome. Risk mitigation can be achieved with additional resources and/or some level of oversight and monitoring.
Low	Low	3-1	Green	Poses little or no risk to success of the intended outcome. If risk mitigation is necessary, it is minimal.

Figure 4. Broad Categorization of Risk Elements.

Figure 4 provides an example of a broad framework within which risk elements can be categorized. Evaluators must be able to accurately assess the level of risk associated with each identified risk element. This can be a difficult undertaking because it requires a thorough understanding of the internal and external operating environments for each identified risk element as well as the necessary technical or contractual acumen. The right data must be collected and analyzed. The involvement of subject-matter experts who possess a solid understanding of the environment cannot be overemphasized. It is the ability to discern "degrees of difference" that guarantees selection of the appropriate risk level. Using ranges of risk, a tolerance band can be an effective way of recognizing margins for error.

Pre-defined descriptors are the broad parameters within which a specifically defined risk element is categorized. Once the risk elements are identified and risk assessment levels are established, risk elements must be examined to determine the appropriate level of associated risk. Figure 5 provides an example with Schedule identified as a pre-determined risk element.

Risk Element: Schedule

Risk Element: Schedule

Schedule Requirement: Delivery 60 days after award of contract. (See Section F of the contract.)

Risk Identification: Sixty-day delivery requirement exceeds commercial delivery standards.

Source of Data: Market research indicates that a 60-day delivery requirement will be difficult to meet. Additionally, a review of 10 recent purchases for similar quantities indicates nine orders were received 3 to 10 days late.

Risk Assessment: High. The probability that the items will not be received on the required delivery date is 93% at a confidence level of .01.

Figure 5. Examination of a Risk Element.

Phase 3: Risk Outcomes and Monitoring

Risk Outcomes. In Phase 3, the findings of the risk assessment are examined in order to identify the consequences. Properly linking cause and effect in this third phase is critical to risk management. If cause and effect are not directly or indirectly related, the risk mitigation plan will be ineffective. Phase 4 involves how the outcomes of one or more risk elements can be interrelated. Outcomes should be clearly defined in terms of direct and consequential effects. The ability to quantitatively characterize outcomes lends additional support to the ultimate decision regarding acceptability of the risk.

Referring to the example provided in Figure 5, it can be noted that the direct outcome is late delivery. There are consequences associated with late delivery. Those consequences may be acceptable or unacceptable. Delivery may be on the critical path, and work stoppage may be a consequence of late delivery. For example, delivery of the items on the scheduled delivery date may be necessary for the start of a new effort.

Risk outcomes must be categorized as either acceptable or unacceptable. Ultimately, all risks must be rank ordered by level of risk, probability of occurrence and categorization. This component of risk assessment is necessary for the efficient and effective utilization of risk managers.

Risk Monitoring. This portion of Phase 3 involves the tracking and evaluation of risk areas. Actual events are compared with planned events to identify possible or real variances. Additionally, the results of the planned events are examined to determine if their outcome is consistent with the predicted outcome. Variance may indicate an unfavorable circumstance, which will trigger the risk-handling phase. Risk handling must be linked to predefined events or milestones so that timely information is made available. These events and milestones should, in turn, be directly related to the Statement of Work. The use of a Work Breakdown Structure (WBS) is a useful method with which to link a work element, event and/or milestone, cost and risk. (For more information on WBS methodology, see Cole, 2003.) A definition of WBS can be found in Appendix A. These pieces of information and their interrelationship contribute greatly to the analysis of risk and prevention of future occurrences. A discussion of Root Cause Analysis can be found in Appendix B.

Risk mitigation is

... a type of

risk control ...

Phase 4: Risk Mitigation

In this final phase of the risk management process, tactics and strategies for risk mitigation must be developed. If the consequences identified in the risk outcome phase are unacceptable from a programmatic or a contractual perspective, a definitive plan of actions and milestones must be generated that will reduce or eliminate the risk. Risk mitigation is, in effect, a type of risk control and is achieved by planning for emergencies and measuring and controlling the identified risks so that appropriate action can be taken. Measurement and control are iterative processes that must continue throughout performance of the contract. In doing so, the manager is better positioned to identify potential problem areas and put the corrective action plan into effect.

An example of a risk mitigation strategy would be the requirement for a performance or bid bond as a condition of bidding. In requiring a performance bond, the public agency attempts to mitigate risk associated with failure to perform by having performance guaranteed by a third party. The following regulatory language provides an example of the considerations for use of performance or payment bonds:

Performance Bonds

(a) Performance bonds may be required for contracts when necessary to protect the public agency's interest. The following situations may warrant a performance bond:

> (1) Public property or funds are to be provided to the contractor for use in performing the contract or as partial compensation (as in retention of salvaged material);

> (2) A contractor sells assets to or merges with another concern, and the public agency, after recognizing the latter concern as the successor in interest, desires assurance that it is financially capable;

> (3) Substantial progress payments are made before delivery of end items starts; and

> (4) Contracts are for dismantling, demolition, or removal of improvements.

(b) The public agency may require additional performance bond protection when a contract price is increased.

(c) The Purchasing Agent must determine the contractor's responsibility even though a bond has been or can be obtained.

Payment Bonds

(a) A payment bond is required only when a performance bond is required, and if the use of a payment bond is in the public agency's interest.

(b) When a contract price is increased, the public agency may require additional bond protection in an amount adequate to protect suppliers of labor and material.

The following clause is an example of contractual language pertaining to performance and payment bonds:

Performance and Payment Bonds—Other Than Construction (July 2000)

(a) *Definitions.* As used in this clause-

"Original contract price" means the award price of the contract or, for requirements contracts, the price payable for the estimated quantity; or, for indefinite-quantity contracts, the price payable for the specified minimum quantity. Original contract price does not include the price of any options, except those options exercised at the time of contract award.

(b) The Contractor shall furnish a performance bond for the protection of the Government in an amount equal to _____ percent of the original contract price and a payment bond in an amount equal to _____ percent of the original contract price.

(c) The Contractor shall furnish all executed bonds, including any necessary reinsurance agreements, to the Purchasing Agent, within _____ days, but in any event before starting work.

(d) The Government may require additional performance and payment bond protection if the contract price is increased. The Government may secure the additional protection by directing the Contractor to increase the penal amount of the existing bonds or to obtain additional bonds.

(e) The bonds shall be in the form of firm commitment, supported by corporate sureties whose names appear on the list contained in Treasury Department Circular 570, individual sureties, or by other acceptable security such as postal money order, certified check, cashier's check, irrevocable letter of credit, or, in accordance with Treasury Department regulations, certain bonds or notes of the United States. (Federal Acquisition Regulation [FAR] (www.acquisition.gov/far/)

Risk management must also consider insurance requirements. Risk mitigation strategies are discussed in subsequent chapters; however, insurance as well as performance and bid bonds are a type of risk mitigation technique. In each case, risk is transferred to the seller. Insurance clauses attempt to provide adequate protection for public agency entities. However, environmental remediation contracts provide an excellent example of the challenges associated with risk management. Consider the contractual requirements imposed in the following Insurance Requirements clause:

Insurance Requirements:

Contractor shall maintain for the duration of this contract, and any extensions thereof, insurance issued by a company or companies qualified to do business in the State of Illinois. The insurance companies providing coverage shall be rated in the Best's Key Rating Guide. The Village will accept companies with a rating of A- or better and shall have a financial size category of VII or better.

1.0   Workers Compensation and Employers' Liability

1.01	Workers Compensation	Statutory Limits
1.02	Employers Liability	
a.	Each Accident	$500,000
b.	Disease - policy limit	$500,000
c.	Disease - each employee	$500,000

2.0   Comprehensive General Liability

General Aggregate Limit	$2,000,000
Products-Completed Operations	$2,000,000
Each Occurrence Limit	$1,000,000

The Village of Skokie is an additional insured on General Liability policy. The Village may accept a separate owner's protective liability policy provided all coverage, limits and endorsements are in conformity with this section. The Village of Skokie is a Named Insured on OCP policy.

3.0 <u>Commercial Automobile Liability</u>—The policy shall cover all owned, non-owned and hired vehicles. The Village of Skokie is an additional insured on Commercial Auto Liability policy.

Combined Single Limit	$1,000,000

4.0 Contractor agrees that with respect to, above insurance, the Village of Skokie shall:

1.01 Be provided with thirty (30) days' written notice of cancellation or material change.

1.02 Be provided with Certificates of Insurance evidencing the above required insurance, prior to commencement of this contract and thereafter with certificates evidencing renewals or replacements of said policies of insurance at least fifteen (15) days prior to the expiration or cancellation of any such policies. Said Notices and Certificates of Insurance shall be provided to the *Office of the Purchasing Agent, Village of Skokie, 5127 Oakton Street, Skokie, Illinois 60077.*

Existing Conditions:

It is the bidder's responsibility to become fully acquainted with the conditions of the work areas. Submissions of a bid will assume that the bidder has included all labor and materials necessary in the bid price to fully complete the work. Construction operations and safety are the exclusive responsibility of the Contractor. (Federal Acquisition Regulation [FAR] (www.acquisition.gov/far/)

It is important to remember that not all low-risk items are acceptable, and not all high-risk items are unacceptable. A low-risk element may be unacceptable; a high- risk item may, in fact, be acceptable. If the late delivery scenario provided in the earlier example is an acceptable risk, a risk mitigation plan will not be necessary. However, if delivery is critical to a planned operation, any chance of late delivery may be unacceptable. In such a case, risk mitigation would be necessary. Alternative risk mitigation strategies may cause other risks to surface. For example, a risk mitigation strategy might include financial incentives aimed at rewarding a 60-day delivery. The risk evaluators must examine the implications associated with adopting a particular risk mitigation tactic. In our delivery example, quality might be degraded in the name of delivery; or perhaps, expedited manufacturing procedures that would result in a 60-day delivery might render the item unaffordable.

Risk mitigation can be expensive. The resources necessary can be underestimated, and the unintended consequences of adopting a particular risk mitigation strategy can be overlooked. Therefore, evaluators should focus on identification of the risk factors while placing a particular emphasis during the monitoring phase on those factors that may impact the achievement of the contract's measures of success.

Conducting Risk Assessment

Initial risk assessment must be conducted early in the acquisition planning stages. Doing so will eliminate costly problems later in the process. Risk assessment is an iterative process, and managers must recognize that the risk management plan can and should be dynamic in nature. A continuous review and assessment of the key program and contract parameters and any attendant risks will serve several purposes:

- Provide assurances that the operating environment is stable and the present risk management plan is valid;

- Confirm that the risk mitigation strategies in place are effective; and

- Identify new risks or previously identified risks that have evolved and require re-examination.

The adoption of an integrated process team methodology is an effective means of conducting risk assessment. Cross-functional team members can make valuable contributions to the risk management process. While the team members share common goals (i.e., successful contract performance and program success), each views the process through a different lens. The team approach to managing risk creates a world that examines risk from competing and conflicting directions. This serves as an enabler to the adoption of practicable risk mitigation tactics and strategies. A "groupthink" syndrome is a detriment to good risk management. Reasoned disagreement among team members should be encouraged as it stimulates creative and critical thinking. (For more information on the use of teams, see U.S. Department of Defense, 1995.)

E-rooms and teleconferencing provide affordable alternatives for adopting and continuing the valuable work of teams throughout the entire contract management process. Regardless of the meeting mechanism selected, regularly scheduled meetings among team members will significantly improve the risk management process. The timing and duration of the meetings will vary depending on size, scope and complexity of the contract and the degrees of risk identified.

Identifying Goals, Outcomes and Strategy

The relationship that exists between program and/or contractual goals and risk must be identified. Each key program and contract parameter must be examined to determine what risks, if any, could impact achievement of the stated goal. The use of a matrix that links key program/contract parameters and the risks that could affect achievement of their stated outcome is a means of marrying goals and associated risks. The Work Breakdown Structure provides a solid foundation for examining program goals and identifying risks that could affect achievement of those goals. Contractual goals and associated risks can be examined by developing a checklist of the critical contract terms and conditions that must be considered. Clearly, adherence to all contract terms and conditions is expected; however, the identification of the critical terms and conditions offers an opportunity for the manager to "down select" to those critical terms and conditions that must be monitored and mitigated. It is not possible to always monitor every element of risk because resource constraints make it impracticable to monitor all program and contract elements. Monitoring of high-risk items with unacceptable outcomes is at the top of the risk management list.

Monitoring of high-risk items with unacceptable outcomes is at the top of the risk management list.

Alternative strategies for ensuring risk management are necessary. While it is tempting to discontinue the search for strategies to manage risk once a suitable one has been identified, teams and managers are cautioned about this practice. Bounded rationality often prevents us from searching for solutions once we have found one that our experience tells us is suitable (Simon, 1948). Consider that other solutions may exist outside the realm of one's own experience. The argument in support of teams is advanced, given this unintended but common phenomenon.

Assessing Levels of Risk

R isk can be categorized as high, medium or low. Risk assessment must be based, at least in part, on an analysis of any interrelationships among the identified causes of any risk. The isolated viewing of a perceived risk prevents the manager from fully understanding all the implications of the risk. The consequence will be development of a risk mitigation strategy that may be lacking.

Subject-matter experts in cross-functional areas are best suited to assess the level of risk. These experts should understand the implications of technical and contractual parameters and assessing the associated risk. Coordination and communication among the team members and the manager will enhance the quality and reasonableness of the initial risk assessment. Any over- or understatement of risk levels will result in unbalanced monitoring and surveillance activity. For example, understatement of risk levels may result in no risk mitigation effort or an ineffective risk mitigation effort. Alternatively, overstatement may result in a risk mitigation strategy that over-utilizes resources because of the difference between the "practical" level of risk and the perceived level of risk. Situational awareness and knowledge of the environment are critical to accurate risk assessment. An understanding of the importance of achieving the stated performance and contract parameters is also a key ingredient of effective risk assessment.

Risk Allocation

The team must determine the appropriate relationships between cause and effect of risk and the rank ordering of the risks based upon level of risk and degrees of tolerance for the risk. Proper allocation of the risk to the stated objectives must be validated. This can be accomplished through the use of Deming's model, "Plan, Do, Check, Act" (Appendix C). As stated earlier, the use of a matrix is an effective means of evaluating and re-evaluating risk allocation. Identifying the key parameters of the Statement of Work and contract terms and conditions and linking the perceived risks helps to ensure that no key parameter has been overlooked. Each key parameter should be examined to ascertain any associated risk. Generally, each key parameter will have at least one associated risk element and may, in fact, have more than one. A risk-free condition is rare. In any event, no key parameter should be presumed to be "risk free."

> *Question for consideration: Can you identify a key parameter that you might consider "risk free"? Explain the dynamics of the operating environment.*

Timing of Risk Assessment

Initial risk assessments should be conducted early in the acquisition planning stage. Ongoing risk assessments throughout the acquisition cycle provide an opportunity to evaluate and re-evaluate the internal and external operating environments and examine the need to update or modify risk decisions. For example, an initial risk assessment for the purchase of crude oil might assess the level of risk for "on time" delivery as low. However, a change in the external operating environment that would create a scarcity of crude oil would require a reassessment of the risk associated with on-time delivery.

During the pre-award stage, acquisition strategies should be reviewed for risk determinations. Early identification of a risky acquisition strategy will avoid problems later in the acquisition process. For example, an acquisition strategy that calls for the purchase of an emerging technology on a fixed-price basis bears associated price and performance risk. During proposal evaluation, risk is an important consideration. The proponent's technical, schedule, cost and other proposed solutions must be evaluated to determine the degree of associated risk. Proponents should be asked to provide their own risk assessment and risk mitigation plan as a part of their proposal. Evaluation of such information can assist in the award determination.

Once the contract has been awarded, earlier identified risks are monitored through the risk mitigation plan. Risk identification that has occurred during proposal evaluation then moves forward into the contract performance phase and forms the foundation for contract performance surveillance and monitoring activities. Regularly scheduled review meetings are an effective means of tracking fluctuations in risk areas. These review meetings should focus on solving problems. Because risk management is a part of the risk management team's daily responsibilities, risk issues are identified prior to meetings; and the meetings are the forums for risk mitigation discussions.

Risk Monitoring

Risk monitoring requires team commitment. Risk monitoring ensures that risks that might occur can be mitigated according to plan. Risk monitoring also helps to ensure that areas of low risk do not escalate to areas of higher risk.

Risk Documentation

Documentation is important in all phases of the acquisition process. Formal documentation of all risk management activities leaves an important "paper trail." The evolving nature of risk demands that documentation be kept current. A database that stores all information regarding a program and contract must include risk documentation. Negative reports avoid any concerns that an area of risk may have been overlooked. As mentioned earlier, the database must have an owner, i.e., a person who is responsible for updating the information. Failure to adopt a formal procedure in which responsibility for updating the database is delineated can result in "at-will" changes to information in the database. Such a situation puts the integrity of the data at risk and may subsequently impact the efficacy of the risk monitoring activities.

Risk and Relationships

Contracts can be grouped into two categories: transaction-based contracts and relationship-based contracts. Transaction-based contracts are characterized by short-term or one-time agreements between the parties. Changing suppliers in subsequent procurements does not jeopardize achieving the stated requirement. An example is the purchase of routine office supplies. Relationship-based contracts are agreements in which the public agency's interests are best served by entering into a long-term relationship with the supplier. The risk balance shifts depending on the category. In a relationship-based contract, the parties may decide to assume more risk than in a transaction-based contract. Care should be exercised to ensure that an unacceptable level of risk is not assumed by one party in order to preserve the relationship. Assumption of too much risk in such circumstances may cause more harm than good.

Striking a balance among the contracting parties that provides for equitable distribution of risk is a risk mitigation strategy. However, the seller may be interested in assuming more or

The public agency can control risk by defining non-negotiable program and contractual requirements.

less than the appropriate level of risk, depending on the characteristics of the relationship. In either circumstance, the public agency must be aware of the type of transaction and its potential affect on risk issues.

As a part of the overall acquisition strategy, the public agency must consider whether the sharing of risk is appropriate. Early industry participation in the acquisition strategy is a means of obtaining the seller's perspective on risk. For example, early market research may reveal that an acquisition strategy for software development that requires Capability Maturity Model (CMM) Level 3 certification by qualified suppliers will significantly reduce the pool of qualified software developers. Such a scenario may have an affect on the price. The public agency acquisition team may have selected CMM Level 3 as a risk-sharing tactic because CMM Level 3 can reduce the risk of software problems. However, industry feedback early in the acquisition process may suggest that reducing the requirement to CMM Level 2 is a better acquisition strategy with acceptable risk. While this move may eliminate a barrier to entry, the balance of risk may now shift from the seller to the public agency.

Methods of Handling Risk

Various options are available to the public agency and the seller when dealing with risk. Four options are generally recognized: control, avoidance, assumption and transfer.

- *Risk Control* is a step taken to reduce the likelihood of an event occurring. These steps are initially identified in the acquisition planning stage and are updated once the contract has been awarded. Risk control options generally involve some degree of trade-off that affects other intended outcomes, utilization of resources and, perhaps, cost.

- *Risk Avoidance* eliminates the risk by removing the requirement or the conditions that may cause the risk. The risk may be the result of immature processes, poor financial health of the supplier or a myriad of other conditions. Risk avoidance can be the most costly of the risk-handling methods.

- *Risk Assumption* recognizes that some degree of risk may be appropriate. Risk assumption requires the public agency (and seller) to carefully and continuously monitor the events that may cause the risk and to implement timely risk mitigation activities.

- *Risk Transfer* shifts the risk either among the parties or perhaps among the other risk or non-risk areas of the program/contract. For example, the use of a "liquidated damages" clause transfers some of the risk associated with late deliveries to the supplier. Or perhaps, interconnectivity between two system parts is high risk due to the use of composite material for one of the items. Redesign may lower the risk and/or transfer some risk to the entire operating system. Such an option may be a better mitigation strategy.

Contract terms and conditions and defined program key performance parameters are the control gates for risk. The public agency can control risk by defining non-negotiable program and contractual requirements. In the earlier example of CMM certification, the acquisition strategy might include a "go/no-go" evaluation of CMM Level 3 certification. In doing so, the public agency controls the quality risk factor by eliminating any seller who fails to meet the stated certification level. The public agency can control risk by imposing additional standards and certifications, in process inspections, Six Sigma (a measure of quality that strives for near-perfection), or ISO (International Organization for Standardization) standards.

Another effective means of controlling risk in the pre-award stage is an acquisition strategy that includes the evaluation of experience and past performance. Evaluating both serves as a key indicator of a supplier's ability to meet program and contract objectives. Experience demonstrates how often the supplier has performed similar work; while past performance is a predictor of how well a supplier will perform, given past history of performance.

The use of an "order of precedence" clause is a risk-control mechanism. Such clauses define the order of the individual contract documents, thereby delineating the rules of contract interpretation in the event of contract ambiguities. For example, such clauses often recognize that the Statement of Work takes precedence over other contract language, particularly "boilerplate" language.

During contract performance, circumstances may arise that cause a contractor to deviate from stated contract terms or performance requirements. Special care should be given to avoid granting de facto deviation. The use of pre-approval clauses that require prior written approval from a designated public agency representative is an effective method of preserving the risk level and protecting the public agency from risky endeavors. For example, suppose that a contract for electronic equipment specifies an exact interface requirement. The contract also permits the contractor to deviate from the stated requirement by using another interface connection. By granting interface deviations without prior approval, the public agency assumes additional risk.

But It Was Only a $500 Job!!

Joe Smiley, Director of Facilities, for the Good Time School District in Snowbank Corners contacted Lilly White, Manager of Procurement for the GTSC. Joe requested that Lilly issue a purchase order to Ralph Fitzbetter, the local steamfitter, to pressure test water distribution lines to the single boiler which provided heating at the Jolly Giant Junior School for $500.00 dollars. This pressure test must be done at least annually.

Lilly agreed to contact Ralph Fitzbetter, make the appropriate arrangements and advise Joe if there were any difficulties. Unfortunately, when Lilly contacted Mr. Fitzbetter and attempted to document the due diligence issues, he advised her that he did not have any General Liability Insurance. Since the GTSC required all contractors doing work for the School District to provide proof of at least $1,000,000 General Liability Insurance coverage, Lilly advised Mr. Fitzbetter that she would not be issuing a purchase order to him for the work, nor could he undertake any work for the School District until such time as he obtained insurance coverage at this level.

Lilly White immediately phoned Joe Smiley and as she attempted to explain the problem, Joe said "I really don't understand why there's a problem here! Ralph has done work for me before and he's a really good guy. I think that making a small contractor like Ralph have that kind of insurance is not necessary and totally unfair. You folks in Procurement are always stopping me from getting work done, and I'm not standing for it anymore. If these kids are freezin' 'cause they don't have any heat, it's not going to be because of me." Joe slammed the phone down.

Although Lilly understood that following procedure and complying with policy could be frustrating for Joe and others, she took the time to e-mail Joe with a complete explanation since she felt it was part of her function to educate her clients and assist them in understanding requirements. She was not surprised, however, when she did not receive a response to the e-mail, nor to her phone call following up on Joe's requisition for the work.

Lilly was eating lunch at her desk the next day when suddenly there was a quick series of loud bangs, she heard people running in the hall, and shouts of "Water! Water!". As she left her office, she saw water pouring out of the ceiling tiles in the hall. She asked a colleague running by "What happened?" and got the reply "Guy working in the boiler room broke a water pipe". Lilly, suspecting what had happened, thought "Oh, no" and took off for the boiler room.

Several hours later, after the main water supply to the school was shut off and most of the flooding had been vacuumed and mopped up, Lilly ran into Joe Smiley talking with the Principal in the cafeteria and overheard Joe say "I don't know how this could have happened. Ralph is a good steamfitter and has never had anything like this happen before." The Principal said, "It doesn't really matter how it happened. It's too late now. Right now I need to know how long the school will be closed and how much it's going to cost to fix this." Joe replied "Ralph says he can have the work done in about two weeks, and he figures materials and labour will cost about $25,000." The Principal looked at Joe in astonishment and exclaimed "You're not seriously expecting me to pay the guy who caused this to fix it! No way. Find somebody else."

Spotting Lilly at the coffee machine, Joe went over and asked if she had any names of any other contractors who had the required insurance from whom they could get a quote. Lilly told Joe to grab a coffee and they'd check her vendor file.

The next afternoon when four contractors met with Lilly and Joe for a site visit, one of the contractors, on viewing the extent of the damage, exclaimed "Boy, the only way you could get this much damage is if you put the system under too much pressure and blew the pipe welds. Only an amateur would do something that dumb."

Questions:

1) Is the value of the work indicative of the risk involved? Explain your answer.

2) Using the risk matrix information from the last chapter, provide a risk assessment for this work.

Summary

E ffective risk management requires a framework within which risk areas are identified, addressed and continuously monitored. The risk management plan must be an active document that is updated through the controlled release of revisions. The use of teams or, if not practicable, the input from appropriate functional disciplines will help ensure that the risk management plan considers all important aspects of performance.

References

Cole, P. S. (2003). *How to write a statement of work* (5th ed.). Sudbury, MA: Jones and Bartlett Publishers.

Simon, H. A. (1948). *Administrative behavior: A study of decision-making processes in administrative organizations* (4th ed.). New York: The Free Press.

Simon, H. A. (1956). *Models of man.* New York: John Wiley.

U.S. Department of Defense (DOD). (1995). *Rules of the road: A guide for leading successful integrated product teams.* Washington, DC: DOD, Office of the Under Secretary of Defense and the Assistant Secretary of Defense.

Chapter 3

Methodologies for Risk Management

Initial risk management takes place in the acquisition planning stage. The use of a risk management database that stores risk-related information offers a centralized approach to managing risk. The database must have an owner so that the integrity of the information is preserved. Information can include: (a) market information; (b) source selection risk information; (c) progress and performance reports; (d) minutes from technical meetings; (e) original risk management plans; (f) revisions to risk management plans and (g) the "watch" list.

Many useful quantitative and qualitative tools are available to assist managers in identifying, assessing and quantifying risk. The database provides a centralized repository of information, which assists managers in staying current about the risk areas and the impact of possible future events. This enables managers to continually examine existing plans and devise additional techniques that may be necessary for dealing with these uncertainties. Of course, risk assessment and mitigation techniques recognize that anticipated and actual outcomes can be favorable or unfavorable. The goal of risk management is to ensure, to the maximum extent possible, favorable outcomes recognizing the cost-benefit trade-off that often influences the risk management strategy.

Risk management tools are grouped into two categories: qualitative and quantitative. The groupings are not mutually exclusive, but each complements the other. For example, teams may prepare "watch" lists and use quantitative measures, such as earned-value management, to manage risk. The watch list may include risk items that have been subjectively identified, and earned value requires some subjectivity because it requires that estimated costs be linked to manageable work elements. Once the estimated costs are linked to manageable work elements, they serve as the baseline for the quantitative analysis, which will help to determine whether actual cost and actual schedule are on target with the planned or estimated cost and schedule.

Tools and Techniques

Market Research

Market research, a critical component of acquisition planning, reveals information about industry trends and specific corporate capabilities. Such information forms the basis for the initial assessment of risk. Market research can be defined as the collection and analysis of information about the capabilities of the marketplace. Information about the marketplace helps to identify some potential areas of risk.

Market research is a useful method with which managers can identify and assess capabilities, trends and emerging technologies at the industry and corporate levels. Informed procurement staff must complete an adequate assessment of the market in the acquisition planning stage. However, market assessment is an iterative process, given the unpredictable internal and external operating environments that exist in the marketplace. Market research can be viewed as a four-step process.

Step One. *Market surveillance* is a top-level environmental scan of the industry. It consists of all ongoing activities that provide insight into trends in the market. Surveillance activities include such routine practices as reading journals, news magazines and newspaper articles that are relevant to the industry. The Internet is also a useful means of obtaining industry information. (See the National Association of Purchasing Managers' Web site for industry trend information. Also, thepaperboy.com provides free access to newspapers worldwide.)

The information gained over a period of time provides important fundamental knowledge that the public agency will need when developing the acquisition strategy. Surveillance is a critical component of market research because it is a long-term "quick look" (snapshot) at the dynamics of the marketplace. Ongoing surveillance activities can alter earlier risk assumptions. When considering a software purchase, the dynamics of the software industry offer an example of how risk assessment could easily change.

Step Two. *Investigation* requires the collection and analysis of information related to a specific procurement action. During this step, the data obtained through ongoing surveillance is applied to the specific procurement.

What is investigation? Investigation includes the identification of potential sources, survey of manufacturers and analysis of responses. In this step, the public agency is gathering specific information about the capabilities of potential sources of supply. Conducting this investigation provides the public agency with important information that puts risk "on the dashboard" so that it is continually examined. As a result, a risk baseline is established and continually reviewed.

Step Three. During *identification*, the public agency should identify the products available in the marketplace as well as the producers. Product identification includes consideration of product characteristics as compared to the key performance parameters and thresholds identified for the requirement. Identification of products and their characteristics will enable the public agency to begin analysis of risks that may be inherent in a specific product or requirement. For example, a particular commercially available product may meet required performance parameters but have a high degree of failure. Or, perhaps, spare parts necessary for the continued sustainment of the product may be only available from the original equipment manufacturer, posing cost risk during the operations and support stage of the life cycle of the product. Considerations may include financing, warranties, reliability, maintainability, and interoperability. A comparative analysis of the commercially available products to the stated requirements can reveal areas of risk that should be addressed.

At the conclusion of step three, the public agency should have completed the following actions:

- Summary of market surveillance activities and information;
- Identification of possible sources and products;
- Comparison of available products to stated requirement;
- Evaluation of possible candidates; and
- Documentation of the market research results and the initial identification and assessment of associated risk.

Step Four. In this final step, the public agency may proceed with the purchase and establish a risk management baseline based upon the information and analysis resulting from the first three steps.

Technical, Contractual And Performance Review Meetings

Technical and contractual reviews will take place prior to and after contract award. However, the composition of the team members will change after contract award when the selected supplier becomes an important part of the risk management team.

Pre-Award Public Agency Team Reviews

As a part of the pre-award planning process, the manager should consider the creation of a centralized risk management team. This team must become familiar with the program, overall contract strategy and the risk management process and is responsible for all aspects of risk management. The team consists of representatives of functional areas/organizations that have a significant interest in the acquisition. The members of the team should conduct a collaborative review that results in a thorough examination of the product opportunities and options and the information obtained through the market research activity. At this early state, such a review includes another look at market research findings and conclusions, which can help avoid costly mistakes. The team writes the initial risk management plan, conducts risk assessments and evaluates risk-mitigation options. Some level of team centralization is necessary to properly categorize risks. This overlap ensures that risk relationships are identified and examined. A decentralized team may be formed in functional categories; however, if decentralization is the choice, the centralized approach to overall management of risk must occur at a higher level. Because teams generate a collective output and the ultimate desired outcome is a well-thought-out risk management plan, the team's end product is better than one that any individual could have produced. The functional representatives on the team view the issues through their functional "lens," which is something that one individual cannot accomplish. Teams must harness their knowledge, attitudes, beliefs and creativity to achieve program success. The following items constitute a model for effective team building:

- Identify the need for a team;
- Organize and staff the team;
- Form and direct team members;
- Develop the team charter and purpose;
- Implement the team charter;
- Provide control for team operations; and
- Disband the team when the goal is achieved.

Team members are tasked with assessing the inherent risks associated with possible product solutions and providing valuable insight into all aspects of risk management. This team will begin the important task of drafting a risk management plan. To effectively implement the team philosophy, the team members must reach agreement in specific areas. Consider the following areas of agreement: (a) attendance; (b) participation; (c) decision-making rules; (d) conflict resolution; (e) expected contributions of functional members; (f) pre-defined assignments; (g) method of communications.

Question for Consideration: What specific ground rules would you establish for teams participating in the risk management process?

The team's collective knowledge will be the major contribution to the decisions that are ultimately made regarding product selection and degree of monitoring and oversight during contract performance. While consensus decision making is the preferred method, risk management requires careful consideration of the decision-making rule. Various functional disciplines will be represented on the team, but all members may not be capable of appreciating the implications and possible outcomes related to a technical risk. Consensus building can take time and requires that team members be educated to some extent about other aspects of functional risk. Alternative types of decision making are unanimous, unilateral and majority.

The consensus method requires agreement of all team members, recognizing that the ultimate decision may not be the preference of all team members. Achieving consensus will not be an easy task. The dynamic exchange of competing and conflicting viewpoints will include spirited dialogue. Hopefully, the success of the program will remain the common goal in that each team member will develop a better understanding of the program, the contract approach and the associated risks. The success of the program must be the primary consideration throughout the decision-making efforts of the risk management team; however, the system constraints cannot be overlooked. Constraints include laws, regulations, policies, resource limitations, etc. Contract risk is a part of the program risk analysis function. The contract is the tool with which the program goals are achieved. Therefore, contractual risk is identified and managed, recognizing that the success of the program is of primary importance. One can put in place the "best written" contract; but, if the program goals are not met, the contract is of no value.

The team must be capable of identifying risk and analyzing the existence, level and likelihood of risk.

Not only is the collection of information that the team gathers and uses of great benefit to the risk management process, it is also the team's continued involvement in risk management activities. The introduction of new team members may be necessary at some point during the acquisition process; however, loss of corporate knowledge can be detrimental to the success of the program. Thus, preservation of this knowledge through thorough documentation is necessary. Ideally, ongoing participation by the same cadre of functional experts is best because it provides continuity during contract and program execution. These experts begin the review process that baselines all acquisition activities.

Risk must be considered through the acquisition planning stage as the team evaluates contract type decisions, required delivery and performance dates, warranty decisions and other matters. Risk continues throughout the source-selection, decision-making process.

> *Question for Consideration: What risks may be associated with a source selection methodology that gives preference to the low bid?*

There is generally some degree of risk that can be associated with a proponent's proposed technical solution, schedule, price or terms and conditions. The team must evaluate the risk and document their findings and conclusions regarding associated risk of a proponent's proposal. The team must be capable of identifying risk and analyzing the existence, level and likelihood of risk. The team should evaluate and assess both proposal and performance risk. Proposal risk is associated with a proponent's proposed technical approach or other elements of a proposal. For example, an aggressive delivery schedule or proposed waiver of operational testing might be proposal risk elements. Performance risk relates to the ability of the proponent to perform successfully. Common performance risk elements focus on a proponent's past performance history and amount of experience.

Considerations should include the following:

- The proponent's proposal as compared to "best practices";
- Unique capabilities of the proponent that serve to mitigate risk;
- The proponent's identification and self-assessment of risk;
- Industrial trends that may alter proposal elements; and
- Experience and past performance of the proponent on efforts of the same or similar size, scope and complexity.

Items such as these should be listed in the risk management plan as areas to be addressed during the source selection process.

Post-Award Reviews

The scope of technical and contractual reviews may expand after contract award. Team members may now include members of the supplier's team.

> *Question for Consideration: What are the perceived benefits of including supplier representative(s) as a part of the post-award risk management team?*

At this point, the baseline document may undergo revision because a risk management plan may be a requirement of the supplier's proposal. In such cases, the supplier's negotiated and accepted risk management plan becomes the baseline document against which risk is examined and measured during contract performance. In performance-based procurements, the supplier's risk management plan is the road map with which the supplier intends to achieve program success. The following are items for consideration in early post-award risk management activities:

- Set up an initial meeting with public agency and supplier representatives to discuss areas of risk; review of the risk management plan; revisions, as appropriate; and approval as the baseline document.
- Conduct a detailed review of the risk areas identified during the pre-award risk-management process.
- Review risk assessments and make necessary changes.
- Ensure that both/all parties have common understandings regarding issues of risk.
- Establish a formal risk-management organization (e.g., team) as specified in the contract or otherwise agreed to by the contracting parties.
- Identify risk-management activities that must take place.

- Identify metrics (e.g., earned-value management) that will be utilized.
- Assign responsibilities among members of the public agency-supplier team.
- Continuously refine and update risk-management plan.

Public agency team members are cautioned that public agency action or direction that alters the supplier's risk plan may constitute a constructive change to the contract. (For a more detailed discussion of constructive changes, see Davison & Wright, 2004.)

Ongoing reviews provide important opportunities to examine progress toward the established baseline and identify risks. For example, progress toward meeting a required delivery date may require risk managers to monitor predetermined events and milestones that must be met prior to delivery. All aspects of risk that were previously identified should be addressed in these ongoing reviews. Additionally, new threats must also be carefully examined. Changes to the internal and external operating environment may alter initial risk management plans. All systems are governed by rules. The deterministic chaos theory states that a small change in a system can create a chaotic response (Chase, Aquilano, & Jacobs, 2001). The result is that a small delay or error can have a dramatic and costly impact on intended goals and objectives.

Routine coordination among functional experts will contribute to successful ongoing risk activities. However, after contract award, the responsibility for the management of risk should be the first line responsibility of the supplier. The dynamics of the marketplace suggest that the character and magnitude of risks can easily change. Thus, market surveillance must never cease.

Progress and Performance Reports

After contract award, progress and/or performance reports are common contract deliverables. These reports must address the risk aspects of the program, including all previously identified risks and newly identified risks that might affect the successful outcome of the contract and program. The framework designated for such reports should only include information necessary for the risk managers to do their jobs. Unnecessarily elaborate reports or reports that contain data instead of information can confuse and unnecessarily complicate the review process, and, reports cost money.

Regardless of the structure and contents designated for formal reports, suppliers must be expected (and required) to include any information that, in their opinion, poses a threat to program and/or contract success. Such information forms the foundation for ongoing risk identification and assessment efforts and may alter the baseline risk management plan that is in affect. Reports should require suppliers to identify the cause of the risk, assess the risk level and probability, and propose risk mitigation solutions. Regularly scheduled reports can provide fundamental working documents that team members can use to analyze the identified threat and analyze, approve and adopt appropriate risk-mitigation strategies.

Watch Lists

The watch list is simply a list of critical items that have been identified as high-risk areas, which should rank order the identified risks by likelihood and priority. The items contained on the list should be those items identified in risk assessment as having greatest unacceptable impact on the program and/or contract. Whether the risk matures or dies, the list provides a quick look at all high priority risk items and should contain a small number of high-risk items. If the watch list begins to grow, it may be an indication that the initial risk assessment was of poor quality. This could indicate that the contract is flawed and that the program is at serious risk because the number of unknowns is unknown. An item that remains on the watch list for a long period of time may indicate an ineffective (or ignored) risk-handling procedure. The watch list should indicate the risk-reduction tactics that have been identified and will be put into action in the event the risk materializes. Other items may be included as a part of the watch list, such as:

- Length of time risk has been on watch list;
- Person assigned responsibility;
- Telephone and email address;
- Risk-mitigation actions;
- Planned completion dates for action;
- Actual completion dates;
- Explanation of the variance between dates; and
- Any other relevant information.

The value of the watch list is its ability to provide current, accurate and timely information. Responsibility for updating risk items on the watch list must be vested with the designated person responsible for the risk item.

The watch list must provide a "quick but accurate look" for those who need to have visibility into risk-management status. Detailed information can be obtained from the individual assigned responsibility for the risk item and from the risk management database.

Root Cause Analysis

Root cause analysis is a relatively simple technique that enables the manager to determine what happened, why and methods of preventing the occurrence in the future. Its primary goal is to prevent recurrence of the same risk during the life of the project/contract. When used with earned-value management, it can prevent a one-time event from becoming a systemic event that causes greater delay and disruption in the achievement of stated goals. Proper marriage of the root cause and direct effect is critical to effectively managing risk. Oftentimes, risk exhibits a domino effect, i.e., one primary cause activates other risk areas.

In order for root cause analysis to be effective it must:

- Involve functional experts who understand the technical aspects of the work and the associated risks;
- Require participation of those experts/stakeholders who are knowledgeable of the situation;
- Involve participants who are constantly probing the environment, continually searching for the "root" cause, which is done by asking "why" in terms of cause and effect at each level of the analysis;
- Involve, through the result of the root cause analysis, the adoption of a process and/or procedures that will prevent recurrence of the problem.

Root cause analysis must examine all factors that could contribute to the problem, including, but not limited to, factors such as environmental, human and procedural matters. The use of a fishbone diagram serves as a simple visual aid in beginning the root cause analysis (Appendix D).

Planning a Root Cause Analysis

Bargain Basement University (BBU) is always stretching their tuition bucks to the limit! This morning the Facilities Manager, Johnny Twelve-Hats was called to the Athletic Facility because of a problem. As he approached the building, Johnny could see that something was wrong. There was water leaking from the front door – thank goodness it was summer and not winter.

Unfortunately the water had also leaked onto the arena basketball floor, but had not yet sat long enough to warp it. The first row of seats along the arena floor had water under them also. Johnny began actively regretting letting the contractor talk him into putting all of the facilities' HVAC and utilities feeds on the second floor of the building in order to save money by taking advantage of the hillside to "embed" the facility, and not haul all the equipment to the lower side.

When Johnny approached the utilities room, he noticed that the floor was dry, and rethought his regret. There were many other sources of water in the Athletic facility. Knowing that there were experts at BBU that could help, Johnny ordered the appropriate staff to clean up the Facility, and then promptly convened a group to help him determine the root cause of the leak and how to permanently fix it.

As the person Johnny admires most, you've been asked to draw up a plan to approach the root cause analysis. Put together a plan that you would present to the BBU experts, and Johnny.

Earned-Value Management

Earned value is an integrated management tool that examines cost, progress and schedule to determine variances from planned profiles (Fleming, 1992). Earned value provides the manager with a means of predicting, with some degree of certainty, actual cost and schedule at completion, given cost and progress at certain intervals of contract performance. Earned value relies on comparison to the baseline cost and schedule negotiated between the public agency and the supplier at the beginning of contract performance. It sets the baseline at the negotiated agreement of progress at stated intervals and the associated budgeted cost. To effectively utilize earned value, the public agency should use the Work Breakdown Structure to break down work elements to their lowest manageable level. (To learn more about the Work Breakdown Structure method of defining requirements, see Cole, 2003.) Once the lowest manageable work elements are identified, the associated costs can be attributed to each level forming the baseline for measuring actual cost and performance against that which is targeted/budgeted. Earned-value information flags risk indicators as well as the effectiveness of risk-mitigation efforts. When variance in cost and/or schedule appears in work in progress, risk mitigation efforts can be examined to determine their utility. When used in conjunction with the Work Breakdown Structure method of defining requirements, earned value offers an effective means of isolating the causes of variances and predicting the impact of variance on total contract cost and schedule. Earned value is commonly used for large-dollar-value contracts that offer cost visibility. Project managers also use it routinely.

Variances

Variance is defined as a deviation from the plan (Lewis, 2000). Variance analysis is a recognized synonym for earned-value analysis; however, the use of the latter term has gained significant international recognition. Managers are cautioned that Earned Value Management (EVM) does not measure or quantify performance objectives, such as quality; other standards must be developed to measure quality. EVM is used to track and monitor cost and schedule.

Figures 6 through 10 provide examples of earned-value analysis. Figure 6 represents a typical cost/funding profile for a project to improve engine performance. Budget is expressed over time. The difficulty with this simple method of examining budget and time is the lack of information regarding level of progress compared to budgeted dollars expended.

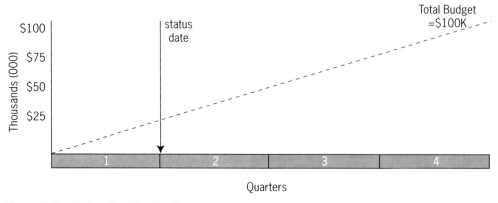

The Project Cost/Funding Plan

In-house Development Project:
"Improvement Engine Performance"

Figure 6. The Project Cost/Funding Plan.

In Figure 7, we see the profile given the first quarter's performance report. This traditional method of examining progress and cost expended suggests that the project is on schedule and under budget.

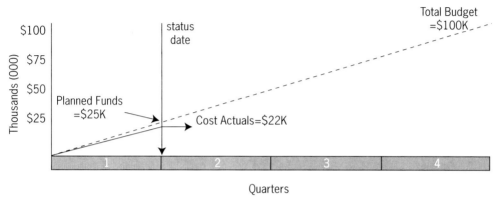

Figure 7. Traditional Cost/Funding Management.

Using the earned-value method, Figure 8 demonstrates the significance of examining the actual cost of work performed to budgeted cost of work performed and budgeted cost of work scheduled to actual cost of work scheduled. These variances provide important information for the risk manager.

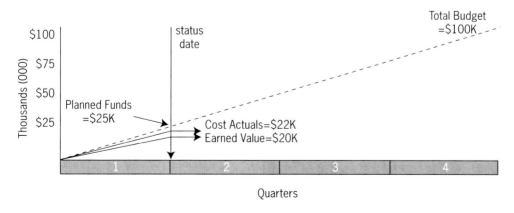

Figure 8. Monitoring Earned Value Project Management.

Source: Fleming, Q. W., & Koppelman, J. M. (1996). *Earned value project management*. Newton Square, PA: Project Management Institute.

We can see that although the actual cost of work performed is less than what was earmarked for expenditure at the end of the first quarter, the actual value of the work completed is less than the costs incurred. Thus, the risk management team is alerted to a possible cost overrun. The reason for the difference must be determined to assess whether it is a one-time occurrence or an ongoing matter. A one-time occurrence, such as a single late delivery by a supplier, does not have the same impact as systemic occurrences, such as unplanned labor wage increases. Isolation of the cause will have an effect on the manager's decision regarding risk mitigation efforts and accurate projections of actual schedule and total cost, given variances.

The Fundamental Difference

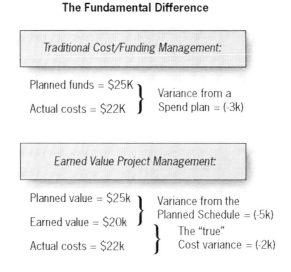

Figure 9. Compares the information that is obtained using the traditional cost model to that using the earned-value approach.

Source: Fleming, Q. W., & Koppelman, J. M. (1996). *Earned value project management*. Newton Square, PA: Project Management Institute.

Applying the earned-value information, the risk manager can predict the "Statistical Range of Financial Cost Projections" by calculating the Schedule Performance Index (SPI) and the Cost Performance Index (CPI). The range represents the low and high ends of likely cost and schedule, given the variances. This allows the manager to assess likely cost and schedule and implement appropriate risk mitigation strategies. In Figure 10, dividing the $20,000 earned value by actual costs of $22,000 yields a CPI of .91 for this effort. In other words, for every dollar spent, only 91 cents of physical work was achieved. Dividing the earned value by the value of the planned work derives the SPI. In our example, $20,000/15,000 yields .8, meaning that for every dollar of work planned, only 80 cents was actually performed. Multiplying the CPI and the SPI provides a composite number that forecasts the high end of the range. Earned-value management has been used successfully in projects/contracts that are in the 10% to 15% stages of completion. Thus, is it apparent that it can be a useful method by which risk managers can anticipate problems early in the stages of a project?

Monitoring Earned Value Project Management

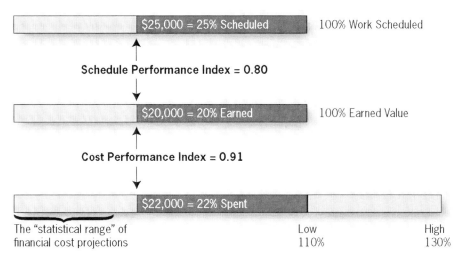

Figure 10. Monitoring Earned-Value Project Management.

Source: Fleming, Q. W., & Koppelman, J. M. (1996). *Earned value project management.* Newton Square, PA: Project Management Institute.

If earned-value management is to be adopted as a tool for managing risk during contract performance, procurement staff should incorporate its requirements into the solicitation and contract. Suppliers should bear the responsibility of providing valid earned-value information as a part of progress/performance reports and should be responsible for providing the range of solutions and the recommended optimum solution that might be appropriate, given the reported variances. (To learn more about Earned-Value Management, see Fleming, 1992.)

Technical Risk and Identification Mitigation Software System

Technical Risk and Identification Mitigation Software System (TRIMS) is used extensively within the U.S. Department of Defense as a risk management tool. While earned-value measures variance in terms of schedule and cost, TRIMS measures technical risk. As shown in Figure 11, TRIMS can be used in conjunction with other databases, such as Best Manufacturing Practices. Doing so enables the risk management team to benchmark against, in this example, best manufacturing practices.

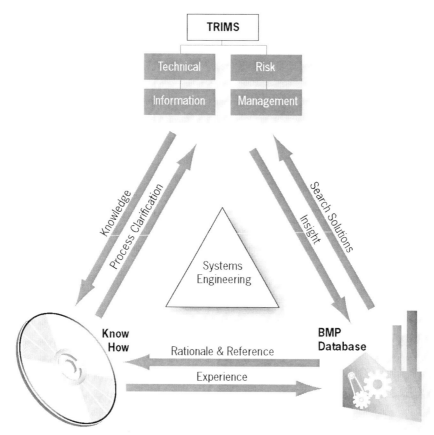

Figure 11. TRIMS as a Systems Engineering Tool

TRIMS identifies areas of potential risk and monitors project/contract goals and responsibilities. Additionally, TRIMS report features allow managers to generate reports to suit specific needs. As with earned value, TRIMS offers the manager an early warning indication of potential problems in meeting targeted goals. A simple mathematical approach to quantifying risk uses the following formula:

$$RF = P + C - (P \times C)$$
Where:
RF = Risk Factor
P = probability of occurrence (0 to 1.0)
C = consequence (0 to 1.0)

Summary

There are many tools available to the risk management team for their efforts to identify and assess risk. The primary goal is to implement one or more of the risk-management strategies identified in the risk-management plan and avoid recurrence of the same problem. Risk management is an iterative process that begins during the acquisition planning stages and continues through the life of the program/contract. It must be continually examined and updated due to the dynamics of the internal and external operating environment. Software tools are available to assist the team in performing this function; however, managers must recognize that software tools only facilitate the risk-management process. No software tool can be a substitute for the exercise of common sense, experience and good judgment.

References

Chase, R. B., Aquilano, N. J., & Jacobs, F. R. (2001). *Operations management for competitive advantage* (9th ed.). New York: McGraw-Hill.

Cole, P. S. (2003). *How to write a statement of work* (5th ed.). Sudbury, MA: Jones and Bartlett Publishers.

Davison, W. D. & Wright, E. (2004). *Contract administration.* Herndon, VA: National Institute of Governmental Purchasing, Inc. (NIGP).

Fleming, Q. W. (1992). *Cost schedule control systems criteria: The management guide to C/SCSC.* Chicago: Probus Publishing Company.

Fleming, Q. W., & Koppelman, J. M. (1996). *Earned value project management.* Newton Square, PA: Project Management Institute.

Lewis, J. P. (2000). *Project planning, scheduling & control* (3rd ed.). New York: McGraw-Hill.

Chapter 4

Developing Risk Management Plans

The focus will now turn to the types of information that should be included in a risk management plan and a suggested format for this plan. Samples are useful in that they offer a starting point for developing a template that an organization can use to standardize the information that should be addressed in their plan. However, samples and templates should not be accepted and used without question, i.e., each risk management plan must contain all the information relevant to each specific acquisition.

Suggested protocol and questions that should be asked as the plan development is initiated are included in Figure 12. A starting point for developing contract focused risk management plans might include identification of (a) key contract terms and conditions that have some associated degree of risk and (b) relationship between those terms and conditions and the required contractual output and outcome. Once these two key points have been identified, the risk management plan can be further developed.

Importance of the Plan

The key to successful risk management is the development and use of a well-constructed plan. The initial risk management plan must be developed early in the acquisition planning stages and continually reviewed and updated throughout the life of the acquisition. The plan becomes the official working document of the risk management team and provides the operating framework within which risk will be monitored and controlled.

A plan should be tailored to the specific acquisition. More complex procurements will require a more detailed plan; while, in more simple procurements, risk management information can be included in the acquisition plan. Regardless of the decision regarding whether or not to create a plan, risk assessment must be conducted. Once the risk assessment has been conducted, the decision can be made regarding the need for a stand-alone plan. The dynamics of the operating environment might necessitate adoption of a risk management plan at a later date. During the monitoring phase, market surveillance, progress/performance reports and other monitoring tools will enable managers to determine the need to revisit prior risk-related decisions.

Responsibilities

The plan should be a team product. Risk is not concentrated in one specific area; a risk does not exist in a vacuum. Also, risk-related events may be interrelated. Often the occurrence of one risk will trigger the second and perhaps even subsequent events. Therefore, using the team approach or soliciting risk analyses from functional areas places the risk manager in a good position from which to monitor risk.

> *Question for Consideration: Identify an area of contractual risk that could be impacted by quality-related risk factors. What might be the relationship between contractual risk and quality-related risk factors?*

As stated earlier, the plan must have an "owner." This individual ensures the integrity of the approved plan and safeguards it from random, unplanned, unapproved changes by well-meaning team members and managers. The owner can be the head of the risk management team or another designated individual. At the very least, this individual should be responsible for (a) maintaining the risk management plan and (b) maintaining the risk management database. The plan is the formal "starting point" because it includes all the risk considerations that have been identified as relevant to the specific acquisition. The team members should agree on common language and meanings for terms used in the plan. Doing so will prevent confusion at a later date. A glossary of definitions is often found in the beginning of risk management plans. This is particularly important if technical terms will be used in the plan and must be interpreted and understood within their technical context.

It is also important to remember that the use of a decentralized approach to risk management requires coordination and integration with the program and procurement staff. All of those who will participate in and influence the procurement process and decision making must be familiar with the risk management plan.

Figure 12 provides an example of the risk management process. Addressing all of these questions will help to frame the content of the risk management plan.

F/A-18 Risk Management Process

Risk: An undesirable situation or circumstance which has both a probability of occurring and a potential consequence to program success; risks are normally associated with uncertainties.
Risk Management: An organized, systematic decision-making process that efficiently identifies risks, assesses or analyzes risks, and effectively reduces or eliminates risks to achieving program goals.

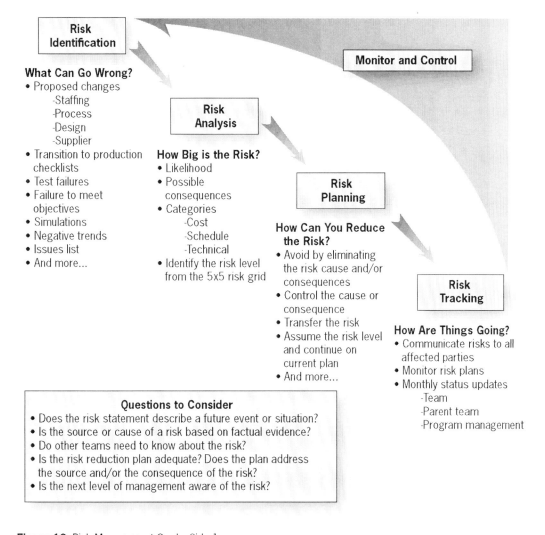

Risk Identification

What Can Go Wrong?
• Proposed changes
  -Staffing
  -Process
  -Design
  -Supplier
• Transition to production checklists
• Test failures
• Failure to meet objectives
• Simulations
• Negative trends
• Issues list
• And more...

Risk Analysis

How Big is the Risk?
• Likelihood
• Possible consequences
• Categories
  -Cost
  -Schedule
  -Technical
• Identify the risk level from the 5x5 risk grid

Risk Planning

How Can You Reduce the Risk?
• Avoid by eliminating the risk cause and/or consequences
• Control the cause or consequence
• Transfer the risk
• Assume the risk level and continue on current plan
• And more...

Monitor and Control

Risk Tracking

How Are Things Going?
• Communicate risks to all affected parties
• Monitor risk plans
• Monthly status updates
  -Team
  -Parent team
  -Program management

Questions to Consider
• Does the risk statement describe a future event or situation?
• Is the source or cause of a risk based on factual evidence?
• Do other teams need to know about the risk?
• Is the risk reduction plan adequate? Does the plan address the source and/or the consequence of the risk?
• Is the next level of management aware of the risk?

Figure 12. Risk Management Card—Side 1.

The plan focuses the team and managers on the areas identified in risk assessment and mitigation. Risk management plans should provide for event-driven decisions that are based on predetermined milestones. Once events occur and risk is examined, meeting-established exit criteria allows performance to move forward in an orderly fashion that is consistent with the plan.

Consider development of a software program that will automate the procurement function, i.e., all documents can be created electronically, released electronically and contract awards can be made electronically with digital signatures. Exit criteria will move this development effort forward based upon the risk identified in each critical software development milestone. Thus, the relationship between risk and progress is an important one that must be expressed in the risk management plan. Therefore, the success of the contract will be determined by the supplier's success in delivering the software on time, within budget and with its required functionality.

Structure of the Plan

The plan must remain current. Failure to do so will render it useless. Material should be organized in a logical fashion that presents the reader with a complete understanding of the risk management issues. An executive overview is worthwhile, particularly if the program/contract will receive high-level management or oversight. The plan should include summary information, introductory information and specific information regarding risk identification, assessment and mitigation. The following sample provides format and content considerations. Appendix E provides a detailed sample plan used for a complex system's procurement.

As updates to the plan occur, an established nomenclature should be used to call attention to the existence of revisions to material contained in the plan. For example, change pages could be numbered as R-1, R-2, and R-3, etc., along with the date of the revision. Doing so allows any reviewer to examine the history of changes to the plan.

Content of the Plan

The following sections should be included in any risk management plan:

Introduction. The purpose and the objectives of the plan should be provided in the introductory section. A synopsis of the program/contract should also be included. The introductory section briefly acquaints the reader with the plan and the organizational structure for managing the risk.

Overview. Provide a brief description of the program and how the risk management issue(s) relates to the program. Information regarding the acquisition strategy, e.g., competitive environment, market conditions, and source selection methodology should be briefly discussed.

Definitions. All members of the risk management team and others who participate in the program/contract decision-making process must share a common understanding of the use and meanings of words and terms. This section should include definitions of the types of risk identified and the definitions for ratings and levels of risk.

Risk Management Strategy. This section should provide an overview of the approach the team will use to manage risk. It should include a discussion of the methods that will be used to identify and manage program/contract progress and related risk.

Organizational Structure. This section should provide an organizational chart that clearly shows the roles, responsibilities and relationships among the members of the risk management team and others who are responsible for the program/contract. Participants should be listed by name with e-mail addresses, telephone numbers and addresses included. The designated responsibility of each participant should be clearly described.

Procedures and Processes. This section is the heart of the risk management plan. It describes the specific tools and techniques that the team has used and will continue to use in assessing, identifying, monitoring and mitigating areas of risk. Describe the procedures that the team will use to update the plan and how information will be obtained to continually re-assess the areas of risk. Planned intervals for risk management processes should be included along with a description of the procedures that will be used to deal with unplanned and unscheduled risk that may interrupt the schedule of events. Metrics that will be used should also be discussed. For example, reliance on earned-value management information, as a means of assessing and predicting risk, would be included in this section. While the procedures and processes should have 'teeth," they should not constrain or prevent the risk management team from adopting a different methodology that would contribute to program/ contract success.

Risk Planning. This section of the plan should demonstrate the structured approach that the team will continuously use to execute an effective risk management program. It should include a discussion of the initial risk-planning efforts and processes used by the team and explain how the team will continue to manage risk. Because risk planning demonstrates that the risk management plan is well thought out, it must include a discussion of the areas of risk that have been identified and a responsibility matrix that links risk areas to managers. Other areas to be addressed should include resource issues that could affect risk management, documentation that is linked to the risk planning process and the tools that the team will use. This section should also address the strategy for updating the plan including a discussion of planned events and activities that will trigger updates.

[The] Procedures and Processes... section is the heart of the risk management plan.

Risk Assessment. This section presents a detailed discussion of the areas of risk that have been identified. The risk assessment discussion should be the most detailed section of the plan. It should address the areas of risk, risk rating and impact of such events; the assessment of probability (likelihood) of occurrence; and the consequences of the occurrence. An example of risk monitoring that would initially be included in the risk management plan is shown in Figure 13. It is updated to show status at a given point in time. Note that as events occur, the updates to the risk management plan indicate that the event is "closed." Closed indicates that the risk no longer exists; it was either mitigated, did not happen (and the project is past that milestone or issue) or happened and was dealt with appropriately.

Risk Management Status

Risk Plan #	Risk Profile	High	Moderate	Low	Status/Comment
94-12-9	Non-stock Listed Spares		▣		Data still in review; need to assign part numbers.
94-12-10	Engineering Updates			Closed	Data reviewed; updates not required at this time.
94-12-11	Spares & Support		→Closed		
94-12-12	Long Lead Requisitions		▣		Spares listing approves in definitization conference. No current abatement plan.
94-12-13	T.O. Validation			Closed	Closed Issue
94-12-14	Lack of LSA Records for GFE		▣		Contractor LSA plan submitted for approval; reschedule for 5/95.
94-12-15	Program Parts Obsolescence		→▣		Analysis in work, identifying last opportunities buys.
94-12-51	Design Maturity		→Closed		Studying Commercial Mux Interface
94-12-16	System Y Interface Definition		▣◄		Questions about antenna location and cable raised risk.

Figure 13. Risk Management Status

Risks should be linked to the relevant areas of the work statement or contract requirement and, in the case of updated plans, include a discussion that links newly identified risk areas that are the result of the proposal evaluation process or a post-award activity. Risk assessment included within the plan must prioritize the risk areas so that risk managers can appropriately focus limited resources to areas of the most concern and greatest probability and consequence. Remember that program/contract risks can have a negative impact on other program and contracts; thus, an assessment of risk as it may relate to interrelationships among programs/contracts is necessary. The following is a list of several key indicators that teams may find helpful in conducting risk assessment:

- Unclear or vague Statement of Work/Specification
- Unrealistic delivery or performance schedule
- Lack of qualified sources or product
- Product immaturity in the marketplace
- Use of Terms and Conditions not used commercially
- Pricing methodology not suited to Statement of Work/Specification

- Failure of a supplier to use best practices
- Non-Compliance with industry standards
- Lack of industrial certifications that indicate process control
- Lack of experienced, available resources
- High attrition rates of necessary personnel
- Supplier adoption of new unproven processes
- Negative industry and/or economic trends
- Supplier offers an unrealistically low price
- Supplier requires financing assistance during performance
- Products fail testing
- Actual schedule lags planned schedule
- Supplier management demonstrates lack of commitment

Because risk management is an ongoing process, the method, timelines and persons responsible for updating risk assessment should also be included.

Risk Handling. The approach and methodology that will be used to manage the risk is addressed in this section. All four types of risk handling, i.e., avoidance, control, transfer and assumption, must be discussed. Feasibility of the proposed method, expected level of success associated with its use and implications on other risk areas should be discussed. Include an explanation of the basis for the adoption of a specific risk-handling method.

Risk Monitoring. In this section, discuss the methods that will be used to continually monitor areas of risk. This discussion should include methods that will be used to update risk status as a result of monitoring efforts. Individual responsibility for monitoring of specific risk areas should be addressed in this section. Alternatively, this section can refer the reader to the Organizational Structure section of the plan.

Risk Documentation System and Database Information: This section includes the last pieces of detailed information that the plan must address. List the contract deliverables and other documentation that will be used to manage risk. Indicate due dates for receipt of such information, content of the risk documentation and location of the stored documents. Address how the documentation will be used and the means with which it will be controlled and utilized to update the risk management plan.

Additional Information. In this section, risk managers should include other information not previously included that is important to the risk management planning strategy.

Checklist

Once it is determined that risk exists and is procurement-related, the need to conduct risk analysis and draft and implement a risk management plan must be addressed. Remember that risk identification and assessment is an ongoing endeavor. For example, little or no risk may exist in the early stages of the procurement; however, suppose that offers are evaluated and none meet the required product delivery date. Schedule risk suddenly becomes a procurement-related matter.

The following list is a model for determining whether risk is procurement-related: Is there risk associated with:

- the requirements determination;
- the Statement of Work and/or Specifications;
- other elements of the procurement request;
- availability of or amount of funding;
- the delivery or performance dates;
- the review process and cycle;
- the release of the solicitation;
- the preferred source-selection methodology, contract type, or competition level;
- the number/quality of proposals received;
- the actions and/or findings of the technical evaluation team;
- the actions and/or findings of the price evaluation team;
- any proposed terms and conditions of any of the proponents;
- negotiations;
- review and approval of a contract;
- the award of the contract;
- the supplier's internal reporting systems;
- quality;
- delivery;
- payment;
- warranties;
- dispute resolution; or
- any other post-award issue?

A "yes" answer to any of the above questions signals the existence of a procurement-related risk.

Identifying Procurement-Related Risks

The Lofty Clouds Airport Authority (LCAA) has always employed and trained excellent security personnel. They have won awards at security conferences and from security experts. However, this force is tremendously expensive to maintain.

Your clients, the airlines, appreciate the great personnel, but have asked for reduced passenger fees (so they can cut ticket prices) in order to attract more flyers to this particular Airport. Competition is fierce between LCAA and a smaller, regional airport which recently reduced the rates they charge the airlines.

The LCAA Board is anxious to meet this challenge and identified Security costs as out-of-line when compared with similar sized airports. Everyone looks to their cost-saving hero, Valus' Add; the Procurement Director, for a plan, including facilitating a risk management plan so that the Board can make an informed decision on this key issue.

Using resources in this Chapter, list the procurement-related risks associated with changing the security function to reduce costs through outsourcing or a reduction in personnel, training, or resources.

Summary

E ach risk management plan has basic topics that must be addressed and discussed. The detailed sections that provide this information must include sufficient information so that the risk management plan indicates a well-thought-out, organized plan that will result in program/contract success. The plan must be reviewed regularly and updated when appropriate. All members of the risk management team must be familiar with the contents of the plan and must bear responsibility for putting the plan into action at the appropriate times.

Chapter 5

Monitoring and Surveillance

Ongoing monitoring and surveillance are necessary throughout the acquisition cycle, and it is important that this effort begin immediately after the contract has been executed. There are various methods for conducting monitoring and surveillance, which range from the non-complex, such as anecdotal evidence gathered while "walking around," to the more complex, such as earned-value management. The method selected should be tailored to the complexity of the requirement and the contract. Grandiose plans for monitoring and surveillance are dangerous because they generally require resource commitments that are outside the capabilities of the organization.

Risk management strategies often fail because the organization lacks the human capital necessary to carry out monitoring and surveillance activities. On the other hand, over-simplification may result in missed opportunities to identify and assess risk. Therefore, an environmental scan of resource availabilities is an important consideration in the development of the monitoring and surveillance strategy.

Dynamics of the Environment

The dynamics of the market vis-à-vis risk management must be assessed and understood. A team approach, which relies on the technical expertise and knowledge of team members, can provide a level of diligence that helps to ensure that no area of risk is overlooked. Technical experts should bring an appropriate level of understanding of the market dynamics to the team. This enables the risk manager to assess risk relative to changing environmental conditions.

The Contract Administration Plan

The Contract Administration Plan is an effective means with which to monitor performance. The plan should be developed immediately after contract execution and include, among other things, a discussion of the risk areas that have been identified. The plan must involve the supplier as well as the public agency team because during the post-award phase, the supplier is responsible for successful performance of the contract. In performance-based contracting, the process used is at the will of the contractor who has been awarded the contract because of its demonstrated ability to perform.

The public agency role should focus primarily on monitoring and oversight, particularly in this era of performance-based requirements. If a risk management plan is developed independent of the contract administration plan, it should include the methods of monitoring and surveillance to be employed by the public agency team. The plan attempts to manage risks. If a separate plan is not used, then the contract administration plan should include a discussion of the monitoring and surveillance activities that will be used to manage risk.

The level of detail contained in the contract administration plan will vary depending upon the complexity of the contract. (For a detailed discussion of contract administration, see Davison & Wright, 2004.) It is important that the plan clearly define the roles and responsibilities of the contract administration team members. Clear definition in this regard will help avoid confusion and duplication of effort, which invariably cause chaos during contract performance. If a separate risk management plan is used, the Contract Administration Plan should briefly outline risk areas and should refer to the Risk Management Plan for further details and guidance.

Performance within the Plan

The Risk Management Plan should include a discussion of the techniques that will be used to ensure that risk is monitored. Risk may be related to supplier proposal or performance. The performance expectations are derived from the contract and the supplier's proposal. Presumably, the performance expectations remain constant unless there is some change to the requirement or the agreement between the contracting parties.

Plan Adjustments

If performance expectations do change, the plan as well as the risk identification and assessment baselines should be re-examined to determine if any changes are necessary. Failure to do so will result in reliance on two documents that do not reflect the revised performance baseline. The result will be surveillance and monitoring techniques that do not parallel the contractual requirements.

The plan-do-check-act model (Appendix C) is a useful means of examining risk monitoring techniques to assess their level of effectiveness. Risk-handling efforts must achieve their desired effects. If these effects are not achieved, the manager must review the identification, assessment and handling procedures and the metrics used and compare them to the contractual goals and objectives. Doing so will help to target possible failure areas. Identification of special events, success criteria and completion of schedule milestones are effective means with which to examine success and shifting risk priorities that may be necessary. As stated earlier, high-risk areas require the most attention. Thus, the metrics and the monitoring techniques employed must be reliable and useful.

The plan-do-check-act model is a useful means of examining risk monitoring techniques...

The risk management process is a continuous process. The plan-do-check-act model provides a closed-loop system in which information can be fed back into the risk management process for evaluation, improvement and enactment of risk mitigation techniques. Low-risk areas should be continually monitored to ensure that they remain low-risk areas. Regular reports will ensure that the risk management system is kept accurate, complete and current.

Identification of the personnel responsible for monitoring and surveillance should be included in the plan. Type and extent of monitoring must also be addressed. For example, if some level of risk is determined to exist on tolerances of manufactured items, random sampling might be a method with which productibility within stated tolerances is measured. Other methods of monitoring and surveillance might include:

- *Data reports.*

- *Random Sampling.* "In statistical terms, a random sample is a set of items that have been drawn from a population in such a way that each time an item was selected, every item in the population had an equal opportunity to appear in the sample" (The Animated Software Company, www.animatedsoftware.com/ascodesc/ ascodesc.htm).

- *Stratified Sampling.* "When sub-populations vary considerably, it is advantageous to sample each sub-population (stratum) independently. Stratification is the process of grouping members of the population into relatively homogeneous sub-groups before sampling" (Wikipedia, the free encyclopedia, www.en.wikipedia. org/wiki/main_page).

- *Regularly scheduled Meetings.*

- *In-process Inspections.*

- *Beta Testing.* "This is a test for a product prior to commercial release. Beta testing is the last stage of testing and normally can involve sending the product to beta test sites outside the company for real-world exposure or offering the product for a free-trial download over the Internet. Beta testing is often preceded by a round of testing called alpha testing" (www.webopedia.com/).

- *Random Floor Checks.*

- *Review of Records* (e.g., attrition rates, labor rate escalation, etc.).

- *Trend Analysis.* "Benchmarking and Trend Analysis provide a way to measure people, processes, technologies, and business practices and strategies against one another. It does this by creating a baseline for quality performance and then tracking performance of all entities beyond that point. Trend analysis may also be useful to see how an entity's performance changes over a period of time" (American Institutes for Research, www.air.org/).

- *Informal Interviews with Appropriate Personnel.*

- *Independent Validation and Verification* (by a third party).

The objective of monitoring and surveillance is to identify risk areas that are escalating or new risk areas that were previously unidentified. Effective monitoring and surveillance places the manager in a proactive rather than reactive situation. (Remember, as a part of risk management plans, methods of mitigating risk have been identified "up front and early" so that mitigation can be implemented when necessary.)

Monitoring and Surveillance Techniques

It's November in Florida – the best time to order air conditioners!!! Oft Flash, the Purchasing Director of the Cheerful Recovery public drug and alcohol rehabilitation facility, is trying to choose which air conditioners to buy. She has bids from seven manufacturers but they are not all equals when it comes to delivery and service after the sale. Uncharacteristically, Oft had left out specifications for delivery, service after the sale, monitoring and surveillance.

Although cooling season begins in March, some of the manufacturers have indicated that significant savings can be had if the units are delivered and installed in May. Further, some offered a 90 day warranty, and some offered a twelve month warranty.

The clients and staff of Cheerful Recovery definitely do need cool buildings in which to recover! Oft decides to reject all bids and revise the specifications. She reads Chapter 5 of "Risk Management" and develops the delivery, monitoring and surveillance specifications. What do these specifications contain?

Summary

Effective and efficient risk management plans should rely on the following:

- Initial and continuous meetings with the supplier to discuss the goals and objectives of the contract and to discuss approaches to managing risk;

- In-depth review of the risk management plan at the initial acquisition planning stage to ensure that the review and assessment is complete;

- Ongoing review of the risk management plan to ensure that new information is examined as it may relate to risk;

- Revision of risk management plans through a centralized control mechanism that protects the integrity of the plan;

- Establishment of reporting requirements and procedures for handling and monitoring risk;

- Continuous dialogue among members of the risk management team; and

- Training that will provide members of the team with the tools and techniques available to effectively manage risk.

Reference

Davison, W. D. & Wright, E. (2004). *Contract administration.* Herndon, VA: National Institute of Governmental Purchasing, Inc. (NIGP).

Appendix A

Work Breakdown Structure

In project management, a work breakdown structure (WBS) is an exhaustive, hierarchical (from general to specific) tree structure of deliverables and tasks that need to be performed to complete a project.

The purpose of a WBS is to identify terminal elements (the actual items to be done in a project). Therefore, a WBS serves as the basis for much of [project planning].

A work breakdown structure is a very common project management tool. Many United States government statements of work require work breakdown structures.

Books

Haugan, G. T. (2002). *Effective work breakdown structures* (The Project Management Essential Library Series). ISBN 1567261353.

Pritchard, C. L. (1999). *Nuts and bolts series 1: How to build a work breakdown structure.* ISBN 1890367125.

Project Management Institute. (2001). *Project Management Institute practice standard for work breakdown structures.* ISBN 1880410818.

Source: Wikipedia, the Free Encyclopedia. Available from http://en.wikipedia.org/wiki/Work_breakdown_structure.

Appendix B

Root Cause Analysis is …?

Root cause analysis (RCA) is a methodology for finding and correcting the most important reasons for performance problems. It differs from troubleshooting and problem-solving in that these disciplines typically seek solutions to specific difficulties, whereas RCA is directed at underlying issues.

- As a process improvement tool, RCA seeks out unnecessary constraints as well as inadequate controls.

- In safety and risk management, it looks for both unrecognized hazards and broken or missing barriers.

- It helps target CAPA (corrective action and preventive action) efforts at the points of most leverage.

- RCA is an essential ingredient in pointing change management efforts in the right direction.

- Finally, it is probably the only way to find the core issues contributing to your toughest problems.

While it is often used in environments where there is potential for critical or catastrophic consequences, this is by no means a requirement. It can be employed in almost any situation where there is a gap between actual and desired performance. Furthermore, RCA provides critical information on what to change and how to change it.

Significant industries using root cause analysis include manufacturing, construction, healthcare, transportation, chemical, petroleum, and power generation. The possible fields of application include operations, project management, quality control, health and safety, process improvement, change management, and many others.

What Is All This Really About?

We form organizations to get work done. As the work we want to do gets larger and more complex, so do our organizations. At some point, we move beyond the capability to function without extensive, potentially complicated processes and systems. These require management. However, we are human and we make mistakes. All the time. Lots of them. Our processes and systems are imperfect, and so is our ability to manage them. We cannot predict the future with any accuracy, and we are unable to see all the potential ramifications of the actions we take. Stuff happens.

In one way or another, all the various management tools and methods that have been developed over the years are about improving how we manage ourselves, our processes, and our systems. We want productivity, we want quality, we want reliability, and we want safety. We want these things now, and in the future. In fact, we want these things to get better over time. This is called continuous improvement.

RCA is about continuous improvement. It is not a pre-defined set of tools and methods, and it is not a flash in the pan management fad. It recognizes that we are going to experience problems, because that is an unavoidable aspect of being human. It is a guiding philosophy that says "find the real, important reasons for our problems, understand why they exist, and change the conditions that create them!"

There are many different versions of root cause analysis in existence, and the differences between them are not always cosmetic. However, I would put forth the following as a general philosophy that is shared almost universally: root causes exist, and they can be found (and uniquely identified) through careful, evidence-based investigation and thoughtful analysis. Finding and identifying root causes during an investigation adds significant value by pointing out significant, underlying, fundamental conditions that increase the risk of adverse consequences. Targeting corrective measures at the identified root causes is the best way to ensure that similar problems do not occur in the future.

Source: Available from www.bil-wilson.net/root-cause-analysis.

Appendix C

Plan-Do-Check-Act Method of Continuous Improvement

Continuous improvement is not a tool or technique as such—more a way of life (or at least a cultural approach to quality improvement)—and the concept of continuous improvement has to be set in the context of 'the quality movement'.

"Quality" as a business issue—in the way we know it now—arose with labour specialization, mass production and automation techniques—techniques, which moved away from the traditional expert craftsman approach to quality.

In the new world of "factories" and mass production, quality was obtained by inspecting each part and passing only those that met specifications. This was true until 1931 when Walter A. Shewhart, a statistician at the Hawthorne plant at Western Electric, published his book *Economic Control of Quality of Manufactured Product* (Van Nostrand, 1931). This book is the foundation of modern statistical process control (SPC) and provides the basis for the philosophy of total quality management or continuous process improvement for improving processes.

With statistical process control, quality inspection of each individual part produced is no longer used—the process is monitored through sampling. Dependent on the results from the sample, adjustments are made to the process to ensure "quality" production.

W. Edwards Deming worked as Walter Shewhart's assistant and protégé and helped further develop this radical approach to improving quality. At about the same time, Shewhart also developed a never-ending approach toward process improvement called the Shewhart Cycle: (also known in Japan as the Deming cycle) Plan-Do-Check-Act.

This approach emphasizes the continuing, never-ending nature of process improvement. The cycle is really a simple feedback loop system.

> **PLAN**—A plan is developed to improve a process.
>
> **DO**—The plan is tested in a small field test.
>
> **CHECK**—The results of the test are assessed.
>
> **ACT**—If successful, the plan is implemented.

The improvement process then begins again and the cycle is repeated. The repetition of the PDCA cycle, with each cycle producing improvement, leads us to the term continuous improvement.

Source: *The Productivity Portal, Index of tools, tips & techniques.* Available from www.lmu.ac.uk/lis/imgtserv/tools/tools.htm.

Appendix D

Fishbone Diagram: A Problem-Analysis Tool

WHAT IS A FISHBONE DIAGRAM?

Dr. Kaoru Ishikawa, a Japanese quality control statistician, invented the fishbone diagram. Therefore, it may be referred to as the Ishikawa diagram. The fishbone diagram is an analysis tool that provides a systematic way of looking at effects and the causes that create or contribute to those effects. Because of the function of the fishbone diagram, it may be referred to as a cause-and-effect diagram. The design of the diagram looks much like the skeleton of a fish. Therefore, it is often referred to as the fishbone diagram.

Whatever name you choose, remember that the value of the fishbone diagram is to assist teams in categorizing the many potential causes of problems or issues in an orderly way and in identifying root causes.

WHEN SHOULD A FISHBONE DIAGRAM BE USED?

Does the team . . .

- Need to study a problem/issue to determine the root cause?
- Want to study all the possible reasons why a process is beginning to have difficulties, problems, or breakdowns?
- Need to identify areas for data collection?
- Want to study why a process is not performing properly or producing the desired results?

HOW IS A FISHBONE DIAGRAM CONSTRUCTED?

Basic Steps:

- Draw the fishbone diagram.
- List the problem/issue to be studied in the "head of the fish."
- Label each "bone" of the "fish." The major categories typically utilized are: The 4 M's: Methods, Machines, Materials, Manpower.
- The 4 P's: Place, Procedure, People, Policies.
- The 4 S's: Surroundings, Suppliers, Systems, Skills.

Note: You may use one of the four categories suggested, combine them in any fashion or make up your own. The categories are to help you organize your ideas.

Use an idea-generating technique (e.g., brainstorming) to identify the factors within each category that may be affecting the problem/issue and/or effect being studied. The team should ask, "What are the machine issues affecting/causing . . .?"

Repeat this procedure with each factor under the category to produce sub-factors. Continue asking, "Why is this happening?" and put additional segments under each sub-factor.

Continue until you no longer get useful information as you ask, "Why is that happening?"

Analyze the results of the fishbone after team members agree that an adequate amount of detail has been provided under each major category. Do this by looking for those items that appear in more than one category. These become the "most likely causes."

For those items identified as the "most likely causes," the team should reach consensus on listing those items in priority order with the first item being "the most probable" cause.

Source: North Carolina Department of Environment and Natural Resources, Office of Organizational Excellence. Available from http://quality.enr.state.nc.us/tools/fishbone.htm.

Appendix E

Excerpts from Risk Management Plan

Utility Helicopters

Prepared by:
_____

Reviewed by:
_____

Approved by:
_____

NOTE: A SAMPLE OF THE INFORMATION RELEVANT TO RISK MANAGEMENT PLANS HAS BEEN EXTRACTED FROM THIS EXTENSIVE PLAN AND INCLUDED IN THE FOLLOWING PAGES.

TABLE OF CONTENTS

Excerpts from Risk Management Plan

EXECUTIVE SUMMARY

The UH-60M Risk Management Plan (RMP) provides a consolidated, documented source for the program's risk information. The RMP describes prior program risk activities and presents the UH-60M team approach for the continuous assessment/abatement and management of risk activity throughout the life cycle of the UH-60M program. The risk management program shall include risk planning, assessment, handling, and monitoring activities to control risk drivers; define risk reduction activity; and provide for the continuous assessment throughout each phase of the acquisition life cycle of the program. Risk management is a key component of the UH-60M acquisition strategy.

Prior to the Integration/Qualification (I/Q) phase of the UH-60M program, the UH-60M Integrated Product Teams (IPT) have incorporated risk management into the overall program management activities to include: 1) leveraging existing UH-60 efforts; 2) establishing a UH-60M performance baseline through trade studies; 3) developing a system-level performance specification and Minimum Commonality Baseline (MCB); and 4) performing an Integrated Risk Assessment (IRA) to establish a program risk baseline. The multi-functional IPT will continue to conduct risk assessment/abatement activities as an integral part of the I/Q phase. The RMP serves as a "guidance tool" for the identification and handling of risks inherent to any acquisition program. The intent of this document is to support program decision making by continually providing updates to the current risk assessment and related risk mitigation activities.

The architecture of the process takes advantage of existing organizational structures; contractual data requirements; and meetings/reviews of informational exchange to develop a disciplined process to identify, assess, document, and continuously update program risk elements. The UH-60M risk management process is a careful assessment of technical concerns and requires the IPT membership's judgment to define the effort required to reach practical solution. The event-driven nature of this approach, whether through technical, cost, schedule, or supportability information channels, ensures that all milestones demonstrate achievement of a practical, producible, and supportable engineering design that meets user requirements.

UH-60м
Risk Management Plan

1.0 INTRODUCTION

The Utility Helicopters Project Manager and the UH-60M Product Manager have established risk management as an integral part of the program management concept. Risk abatement/management is a continuous, pro-active process that concentrates on early identification and control of program risk areas. Program areas are evaluated in terms of technical performance, cost, schedule, producibility, and supportability to address the total system and considering life cycle impacts.

1.1 SCOPE

The UH-60M Risk Management Plan (RMP) details the risk management approach; describes prior risk reduction activities; quantifies the known and potential risk areas within the program; and documents continuous risk control, handling, and reduction efforts. The integrated risk management approach has four major components as described herein:

- Planning
- Assessment
- Handling
- Monitoring

The RMP serves as a "guidance tool" to enhance the Integrated Product Team (IPT) structured approach to integration, qualification and test, production, and fielding activities in their efforts to reduce the inherent risks of system integration, producibility, and supportability.

(NOTE: Detailed content in specific sections not germane to specific risk management discussion is deleted.)

Risk management in all areas of the UH-60M program has been a central focus of activity.

3.1 I/Q DEFINITION/RISK REDUCTION

The risk reduction efforts of the UH-60M program began early with user and contractor involvement to maximize efficiency and minimize risk of not meeting requirements. I/Q Definition activities include the following:

- Integration of Existing UH-60 Efforts
- Trade-Off Analyses
- Performance Specification/MCB
- IPT Approach

- MS I/II
- Integrated Risk Assessment
- Combined Test Team

1.4   IPT APPROACH

The early establishment of the IPT process was paramount in ensuring the successful implementation of "continuous" risk management. The UH-60M program will be managed through the IPT management structure shown in Figure 4. The Government, Contractor, User, and supporting Government agencies are represented.

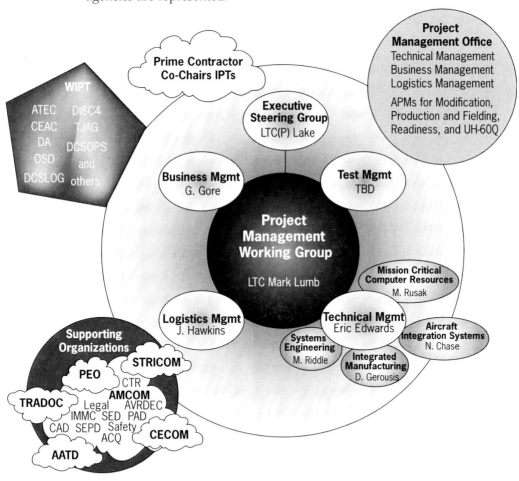

Figure 4. UH-60M Program IPT Structure

4.0   RISK MANAGEMENT METHODOLOGY

The basic strategy of the UH-60M risk management approach is to identify critical areas and risk events, both technical and non-technical, and take necessary actions to prevent cost, schedule, and/or performance impacts. The IPTs serve as the key focal point for accomplishing risk management activities and performing the risk management process. This approach allows the UH-60M program to gain multi-functional information from team members with functional expertise in all areas.

Integrated risk management efforts focus on monitoring and managing program elements which may impact the success of the program by utilizing technical performance measurement, cost, and schedule tools, in existence and in use by the PM and the Contractor. Identification of these areas through the IPT process may result in further evaluation of the risk management process and the identification of new risk elements. The continuous feedback and update cycle of the RMP provide the UH-60M program with the means to predict future resource requirements, as well as manage near term goals.

The risk management process identifies a hierarchy of risks that may potentially impact the successful achievement of program goals, objectives, thresholds, and/or established program milestone exit criteria. For consistency throughout the program, the risk level definitions in Figure 5 have been developed.

RATING	TECHNICAL	SCHEDULE	COST	SUPPORTABILITY
Low	Previously demonstrated technology Requires integration and testing Manageable within PM's discretion	Plans and forecasts indicate successful accomplishment of milestone within 10% of planned schedule	Actuals plus forecasts indicate completion within < 10% growth of anticipated costs	Likely to meet supportability requirements
Moderate	Prototype technology demonstrated Design iterations and testing required Potential serious impacts, but manageable within current requirements	Plans and forecasts indicate a potential of >10%; but <20% additional schedule growth may be required	Actuals plus forecasts indicate >10% but ≥ 20% growth of anticipated costs Manageable within current management reserves	Possible support constraints or deficiencies Sustainment cost constraints
High	Concept and/or technology not demonstrated Current analysis not conclusive Potential major impact that would require program restructure and/or revision of requirements	Plans and forecasts indicate a potential of >20%; additional schedule resources may be required	Actuals plus forecasts indicate >20% growth of anticipated costs Resources required exceed management reserves	Potential major impact on supportability

Figure 5. Risk Level Definitions

4.1 RISK MANAGEMENT EXECUTION

Risk Management for the UH-60M program is accomplished as an integral part of the program management function. Risk is addressed as a single entity consisting of technical, cost, schedule, and supportability throughout the entire program life cycle. The elements of the risk management approach and the general guidelines for each element are described in subsequent paragraphs.

4.1.1 Risk Planning

The RMP serves as the basis for all detailed risk planning, which is a continuous, integral part of normal program planning and management of the UH-60M program. The RMP provides IPTs with an organized approach to assess, handle, and monitor risks while assigning responsibility for specific risk management actions. Each IPT will perform the actions listed:

- Each IPT will develop a thorough approach to assess, handle, and monitor risks. Actions will be assigned for specific risk management activity and internal reporting and documentation procedures will be maintained. The PMWG will ensure that all IPT activities are consistent with this RMP and that appropriate revisions to this plan are made as required.

- Each IPT will report risk status to the Risk Manager on a scheduled timely basis.

- Each IPT will maintain risk information in the Risk Management Database to be used by the Government and the Contractor.

- Each IPT will establish metrics to measure the effectiveness of selected risk handling options. See documents in Section 1.2 for further guidance and sample metrics.

- Each IPT will identify resource requirements to implement risk management actions to include time, material, personnel, and cost.

- Training is a major consideration. The PMWG will arrange general risk management training and IPT leaders should identify any specialized training requirements.

4.1.2 Risk Assessment

Risk Assessment consists of the identification of critical risk events/processes, the analyses of these events/processes to determine the likelihood of occurrence/process variance and consequences, and the priority of the risks. The risk assessment process consists of four steps:

- Identification

- Analysis

- Rating

- Prioritization

It is essential that all areas of the UH-60M program be analyzed for potential risk areas, since the output of the risk assessment will provide the foundation for risk handling activity.

Risk assessments will be performed by each IPT and the PMWG with active participation from both Government and Contractor personnel. IPTs will continually assess the risks in their areas, reviewing critical risk areas, risk ratings and prioritization, and the effectiveness of risk mitigation actions when necessary. The assessment process will be iterative with each assessment building upon the results of previous assessments. IPTs will utilize the Integrated Risk Assessment (IRA) as the baseline and a starting point for their efforts during the I/Q phase. The IRA is an assessment developed by the UHPMO in support of the MS I/II decision. Risk assessments from the IPTs will be updated by the Risk Manager and results presented at all functional and program reviews, with a final update for this phase prepared no later than six months prior to MS III.

1.1.1.1   Identification

Identification is the first step in the risk assessment process.

The basic process involves searching the UH-60M program to determine those critical events that may prevent the program from achieving its objectives. Risks will be identified by each IPT through application of knowledge, best judgement and experience, lessons learned from similar programs, and subject-matter experts (SMEs). Following are the general procedures for risk identification:

- Understand the requirements and program performance goals.
- Determine technical/performance risks related to engineering and manufacturing processes.
- Determine technical/performance risks associated with the product in the critical areas.
- Identify cost, schedule, and supportability issues/risks.

1.1.1.1   Analysis

Risk analysis is an evaluation of the identified risk events to determine the likelihood of the events occurring and their consequences, to assign a risk ratings based on the program criteria, and to prioritize risks. Each IPT is responsible for analyzing those risk events that they identify. Techniques to support risk analysis include trade studies, test results, modeling and simulation, expert opinion, system engineering analysis, risk assessments, or any other accepted analysis technique. The risk analysis process involves:

- Identification of Work Breakdown Structure (WBS) elements.
- Evaluation of WBS elements using the risk areas to determine risk events.
- Assignment of likelihood/probability and consequence to each risk event to establish a risk rating.
- Prioritization of each risk event relative to other risks.

  Each IPT will evaluate each risk event in terms of consequence to technical performance, schedule, cost, supportability, or impact to other IPTs and assign a level for the consequence. Figure 6 will be used when assigning values for likelihood/probability and consequence to risk events.

THE RISK ASSESSMENT PROCESS

Likelihood:

Level	What Is The Likelihood The Risk Will Happen?
a	remote
b	Unlikely
c	Likely
d	Highly Likely
e	Near Certainty

ASSESSMENT GUIDE

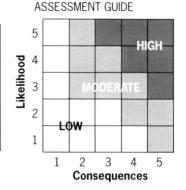

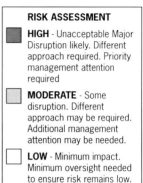

RISK ASSESSMENT

HIGH - Unacceptable Major Disruption likely. Different approach required. Priority management attention required

MODERATE - Some disruption. Different approach may be required. Additional management attention may be needed.

LOW - Minimum impact. Minimum oversight needed to ensure risk remains low.

Consequence: Given the Risk is Realized, What is the Magnitude of the Impact?

Level	Technical Performance	and/or	Schedule	and/or	Cost	and/or	Impact on Other Team
1	Minimal or No Impact		Minimal or No Impact		Minimal or No Impact		None
2	Acceptable with Some Reduction in Margin		Additional Resources Required; Able to Meet Need Dates		<5%		Some Impact
3	Acceptable with Significant Reduction in Margin		Minor Slip in Key Milestone; Not Able to Meet Need Dates		5-7%		Moderate Impact
4	Acceptable, No Remaining Margin		Major Slip in Key Milestone or Critical Path Impacted		>7-10%		Major Impact
5	Unacceptable		Can't Achieve Key Team or Major Program Milestone		>10%		Unacceptable

NSSN Risk Process Card- February 1996

Figure 6. Risk Assessment Process

1.1.1.1   Rating

Each identified risk will be assigned a risk rating based on the consideration of event likelihood and consequence. This rating is a reflection of the severity of the risk and provides a starting point for the development of risk handling options. Risk events that are assigned a MODERATE or HIGH rating by an IPT will be reported to the Risk Manager for submission to the PMWG for active management involvement. Other risk events will be continuously assessed to maintain currency of risk ratings.

1.1.1.2   Prioritization

MODERATE and HIGH risks will be prioritized within each IPT area. This will provide the basis for the development of risk handling plans and the allocation of resources. The PMWG will review the prioritized lists of the

IPTs and integrate into a single list of prioritized program risks, using the same criteria.

4.1.3 Risk Handling

For all risks identified, risk handling methods must be developed by the IPTs. The handling techniques should be evaluated in terms of feasibility, expected effectiveness, cost and schedule implications, and the effect on system technical performance. Reduction of requirements as a risk avoidance technique will be used only as a last resort, and then only with participation and approval of the user's representative. Evaluation of risk handling techniques should consider the following:

- What must be done;

- List of all assumptions;

- Level of effort and material required;

- Resources required that are outside scope of contract;

- Estimated implementation cost;

- Proposed schedule in relation to Program milestones;

- Recommended metrics for tracking;

- Other areas of impact;

- Person responsible for implementing option.

Risk handling methods will be integrated into program planning and scheduling. IPTs will develop these actions and events in the context of the WBS elements, establishing links between them and specific work packages to simplify determinations of impact on cost, schedule, supportability, and performance.

4.1.4 Risk Monitoring

Risk monitoring is the systematic tracking and evaluation of the progress and effectiveness of risk handling actions by the comparison of predicted results of the planned actions with the results actually achieved. The status of the risks and the effectiveness of these actions will be agenda items for all functional and program reviews, and will be reported to the PMWG on a monthly basis or as requested.

4.2 RISK MANAGEMENT ORGANIZATION

The implementation of the risk management process takes advantage of planned organizational structures, program reviews/meetings, chartered IPTs, and information flow. The risk management process organization directly correlates with the established IPT structure that allows risk management to proceed up from the IPTs to the PMWG. Risk elements are assessed for both criticality to program objectives and effect on overall program execution.

The IPTs are the focal point for the established risk management process.

Working Groups may be established as subsets of these IPTs if required. The IPTs are chaired by the appropriate individual who is responsible to both the UHPMO and the UH-60M Product Manager for a particular area. The IPT Leaders are responsible for all technical performance, cost, schedule, and supportability aspects of his/her assigned area. The IPT members are comprised of functional area representatives, supporting SMEs, user representatives, and contractor personnel. The goal of these IPTs is to identify, evaluate, and resolve issues at the working level. If issues cannot be resolved at this level, options will be formulated and presented to higher management for resolution and/or decision.

3.3   RISK MANAGER

The System Engineering/Performance (SE/P) IPT will serve as the program Risk Manager. The function of the Risk Manager will be to track and maintain a database of all risks identified by the IPTs. The Risk Manager will develop the PM Watchlist for the UH-60M program. The Risk Manager will work concurrently with the Contractor to maintain the UH-60M Risk Management Database for utilization by all IPTs and supporting personnel.

4.4   PM WATCHLIST

The PM Watchlist presents risk areas and associated risk elements for the PMWG recommended for inclusion by IPT leaders. Bulletized rationale for their risk ratings are presented with more in-depth analysis available at the IPT level. This Watchlist consists of those risk areas rated as MODERATE OR HIGH by the IPTs. The PMWG will prioritize the list of these high risk areas based on overall program objectives and resource availability.

5.0   I/Q RISK MANAGEMENT

Essential to the overall UH-60M risk management approach is the integration of cost and schedule analyses with the technical performance analyses to provide the program with the following key objectives:

- Provide accurate, "cross-walked" cost and schedule status of identified risk elements.

- Provide early warning of cost and schedule issues to allow prioritization of available resources.

- Forecast future cost and schedule status based on current technical performance, remaining scope of work, and available resources.

5.1   COST MANAGEMENT

The cost management methodology implemented as a part of this risk management program includes planning, baselining, and assessment activities. The BLACK HAWK cost management program provides a solid baseline for contractor and Government performance measurement, a Cost/Risk Watchlist, early warning for identifying problem areas, and an integrated team approach to cost control and management of program risks. Cost management is enhanced through the use of a Cost Plus Award Fee (CPAF) contract to provide motivation for excellence in contract performance. Award fee will be based on increases in performance and/or reliability, increases in the level of cockpit digitization, and reductions in O&S costs. Contractor costs will be closely monitored through an EVMS for early detection of cost growth and program adjustments will be made as necessary to control costs. The contractor will be required to conduct a Depot Partnership Study to determine the cost/benefit impacts of a contractor/depot partnership arrangement during the Full Rate Remanufacture/Production phase. Study recommendations will be used to evaluate best value options for the Army prior to Full Rate Remanufacture/Production. Funding requirements necessary for program execution have been identified and requested through the appropriate program planning channels.

5.1.1 PLANNING

The objective of the planning process is to ensure that the program cost risk elements and associated cost goals are addressed early to provide an accurate baseline for monitoring and controlling risk elements. Cost goals will provide the "means for measurement" milestones for risk elements. Existing data from contractor and Government models, systems, and reviews will be the basis used to produce a comprehensive database for program performance analysis. Deficiencies in baseline data will be identified during this phase.

During the planning phase, the accuracy of the systems, models, and analyses used in the program will be determined (e.g., the accuracy and consistency of schedules and cost performance data). The data sources will be monitored to ensure that future analyses will be based on informed judgment rather than blind acceptance of every data source. A "cross-walk" of risk elements to cost performance data and scheduling will be fairly straightforward if these systems provide an accurate picture of program progress based on the technical performance risk. The BLACK HAWK team personnel will continually monitor the systems, models, and processes being used in "cross-walk" efforts to assure the quality of the resulting analyses.

As part of cost planning, the RFP includes requirements to provide the Government with cost performance data available through the IPT process and via the Contractor Integrated Technical Information Service (CITIS). Program and financial management shall include: reviews, event-driven program scheduling and networks, WBS implementation, EVMS implementation, subcontractor management, life-cycle cost estimation, and use of Continuous Acquisition and Life-cycle Support (CALS) processes. The contractor shall utilize the EVMS to plan, budget, and implement a financial management program to control the resources allocated to meet the requirements of the UH-60 Modernization Program. The contractor is also required to CAIV throughout the program using an integrated total life cycle approach to provide an affordable, producible, and sustainable design in accordance with the system performance specification, AVNS-PRF-10002.

The following are some examples of "cross-walks" that may be used to determine variances in performance, analyze the cause and effects, project future program impacts, and allocate resources to mitigate or resolve existing or potential issues:

- Project Office Estimate (POE) versus Contract Proposal

- Schedule versus Performance Measurement Baseline (PMB)

- Earned Value versus Schedule Status

- Government versus Contractor Life Cycle Cost (LCC) Estimating Methodologies

Review of these items will ensure that the proper linkage exists between development, production, and operating and support cost elements. Plans identifying Government Furnished Equipment (GFE), facilities, and personnel will be reviewed to ensure that all contractual efforts and requirements are addressed. Once completed, contractor performance can be accurately assessed against a single program baseline.

5.1.2 BASELINING

The management baseline consists of a PM Watchlist (i.e., a prioritized list of the highest risk elements as described below), PMB, and current Program Management Network (PMN) schedules. The programmatic database will aid in determining if a risk element will be placed on the PM Watchlist or relegated to a lower level of management. The baseline provides a foundation for analysis of program performance. An IBR will be conducted within 180 days after contract award and establishment of the baseline. The purpose is to review the contractor's cost and schedule performance baseline, specifically the technical, resource, and schedule plans. Periodic independent Government Estimate At Completion (EAC)

Reviews may continue throughout the life of the contract, especially when significant detailed planning is done or after major contract decision milestones have been reached. In these cases a new IBR may be appropriate. The IBR will validate the following:

a. The PMB is valid and work flow-down is consistent between the contract SOW and work authorization documents.

b. The technical content of cost accounts and work packages derived from the SOW is reflected in program changes and has sufficient resources.

c. The scheduling system is integrated with the performance measurement baseline and schedule milestones, and activities must be logically sequenced and time-phased and key interdependencies identified.

d. The contractor is using appropriate performance measurement techniques (special attention is given to ensuring that the contractor is using measurement techniques that will provide effective, objective performance information).

e. The EAC procedures are in place, and Cost Account Managers (CAMs) understand the process.

f. The contractor is managing subcontractors' cost, schedule, and technical performance and that subcontractor data flows properly into the prime contractor's system.

g. High-risk areas of cost, schedule, and technical performance are identified and monitored. Corrective actions generated from the IBR are monitored by the appropriate IPT until final resolution.

5.1.3 ANALYSIS

Analysis involves examining contractor data relative to a risk element to as low a level as is both practical and possible (work package level). Upon establishment of a valid Contract Budget Baseline (CBB), a monthly assessment of contractor cost and schedule data will be performed. Cost Performance Reporting (CPR) will contain contractor cost and schedule performance information. Controlling will require the monitoring of contractor or subcontractor cost accounts. Through the in-depth examination of cost accounts, work packages, WBS data, a greater understanding of technical performance, cost, and schedule program risk will be achieved.

5.1.3.1 EARNED VALUE ANALYSIS

Earned value analysis will be viewed as a business management tool that will result in an efficient, optimized, successful program. Earned value procedures are essential in identifying "early warnings" of problems. They can depict where the problem is, how much it is costing in time and money, and provide a prediction for the cost at completion.

All programmatic tools will be similarly mapped to ensure information is available and can be associated with appropriate outputs from other systems. This ensures that all technical performance, cost, and schedule issues are included in the different reporting systems used by the project office and the contractor. The IPT will apply this data to the risk elements for proper risk assessment.

The information obtained during the analysis process will be presented to the appropriate IPT Leader on a monthly basis to augment other technical performance, cost, and schedule reports. Data developed from monthly cost account analyses is summarized in text and graphic format for BLACK HAWK managers. The data provides technical and business staff with timely information which is crucial in such areas as technical interchange, rationale for decision making, validation of cost/schedule trends and forecasts, and as a basis for potential work-around plans to mitigate identified risks. Monthly cost management reviews are conducted which include an overview of program status in terms of cost and schedule trends, LCC; and, a focus on program risk elements and other resource drivers, as well as, on required management actions. The review provides senior management with a summary of monthly integrated cost analysis from such activities as cost reporting analysis, risk management assessments, I/Q program activities, CAIV program, program funding execution, and review of open action items.

Areas of emphasis for cost account analyses will vary throughout the life of the program. The process employed within the UH-60 Modernization Program is flexible and robust enough to accommodate changes in known or potential risk areas.

5.2   SCHEDULE MANAGEMENT

Event-driven risk reduction schedules, program schedules, and the PMN are an integral part of the risk management process. The same basic phases, planning, baselining, and analysis, of cost management are applicable to schedule management.

5.2.1 PLANNING

The objectives for the schedule management planning phase are to identify critical goals for successful program execution and to ensure the technical program is adequately scheduled. The programmatic schedule tools that are used to focus management activities on identified risk elements are selected program schedules, event-driven risk reduction schedules, and the PMN.

The PMN illustrates the planned activities and logic necessary to successfully accomplish the SOW. A three-level hierarchy of program milestones will be created to facilitate analysis and communication among IPT members. In keeping with the risk management methodology, Level I Milestones are controlled by the UH-60 Modernization Product Manager and reflect those critical events which are necessary for the overall successful completion of the program as defined by the Acquisition Program Baseline. Level II and III Milestones are established by the contract and are controlled by the appropriate lower level manager to attain Level I goals. Each milestone is specifically defined with a minimum of information consisting of:

• <u>Planned Date</u>:   Agreed to date for the completion of a milestone. The planned dates constitute the program schedule baseline.

• <u>Milestone Description</u>:   The technical performance requirements necessary to successfully complete the milestone.

In the PMN, program milestones are logically linked and appropriately constrained by planned activities. Changes to the planned dates or descriptions for Level II and III Milestones are only made with the formal approval of the Product Manager.

5.2.2 BASELINING

The establishment of a PMB assures that a detailed program schedule is established which addresses milestones for identified risk reduction activities. Activities, durations, and dates establish the baseline. The primary purpose of the PMN is overall program planning and status; however, the PMN is directly linked to lower level schedules and planning data, down to and including, individual cost accounts and work packages. This linkage provides the means for ensuring that the sequence and flow of tasks support the overall program plan. The contractor is required to provide schedules and planning data to the Government via the CITIS.

The identified risk reduction milestones are quantified as to the risk reduction value expected upon successful completion. Each IPT Leader is responsible for reviewing the milestones and ensuring that what is shown in program schedules accurately reflects their risk concerns as the program progresses through time.

5.2.3 ANALYSIS

Analysis of schedule and cost allows the project office to document the history of the program and apply actual cost and schedule experience to: 1) project future technical performance requirements and risk reduction activities in terms of time and money, 2) provide a measure against the APB, and 3) project what milestones will be missed due to cost and schedule anomalies.

Milestone trend charts, critical path analyses, and overall program status, as measured to identified milestones, provide independent checks and balances to ensure that program risk elements have been identified and sufficient resources are available to accomplish the events. The following are useful network tools to aid in analyzing risk items:

- Number of Milestones Planned versus Number of Milestones Missed over Time

- Milestones 30/60/90 Days Late

- Duration Reductions of Future Activities

- Input and Output Listing at the Cost Account Level

- Recovery Plan Logic Check

A "cross-walk" of identified risk elements to the associated cost accounts and supporting schedules is conducted. Databases can be developed to link PMN activities with identified risk reduction events and used for performance measurement and an assessment of the man-hours and costs associated with accomplishing these events.

Monthly man-hour and cumulative man-hour data will be used to facilitate the IPTs' ranking of risk drivers at the WBS or Work Package Level. This data will be able to be updated on demand to support on-going risk assessments and used to verify analyses performed by the IPTs.

5.3   SUPPORTABILITY MANAGEMENT

Supportability is a principal design and program requirement as important as cost, schedule, and performance. It will be a primary factor in all program and budget decisions, trade-off analyses, tests and evaluations, and other program events in the acquisition process. Supportability will be managed by employing the same processes used to manage cost, schedule and performance (planning , baselining, and analysis). The supportability management process will identify risks and mitigation activities within the Integrated Logistics Support (ILS) elements (maintenance planning, manpower and personnel, supply support, equipment support, technical data, training and training support, computer resources support, facilities, packaging, handling, storage, and transportation (PHS&T), and design interface) to ensure that all ILS requirements are accomplished during acquisition and support of the UH-60M.

5.3.1 PLANNING

The principal objectives of Supportability Planning are: First, to influence the materiel design for logistics purposes and to define the support requirements reflected by the design. The Second objective is to develop the support and provide that support to the Army in the field by controlling risk elements. Early in the planning phase, the Supportability Team will identify specific goals and objectives of the ten ILS elements to meet the user's requirements as defined in the ORD and System Training Plan (STRAP). Tradeoffs between elements will be conducted in order to establish a system that is affordable (lowest LCC), operable, supportable, sustainable, transportable, and environmentally sound within the resources available. MANPRINT is an integral part of all ILS elements and will be addressed in each element. ORD and STRAP requirements will be translated into the Supportability Strategy, a document outlining the strategy for supporting the UH-60L+ throughout the life cycle. These three documents serve as the foundation for supportability requirements found in the SOW and the System Specification. IPT processes, milestones and in-process reviews, system readiness reviews, documentation reviews, and training readiness reviews will be defined and instituted.

5.3.2 BASELINING

The Supportability baseline will consist of the risks associated with each ILS element, the mitigating activities associated with each risk, and a schedule (agreed to through the IPT process) indicating the milestones for publications review, publications verification/validation, training conference reviews, logistic demonstration, etc. The baseline provides a foundation from which the contractor's effort in terms of the ten ILS elements may be measured and analyzed. Cost and schedule management will tie into the supportability baseline as shifts in either may affect ILS risk. The Logistics IPT will be responsible for reviewing ILS activities to ensure activities are being performed per the plans and deliveries are made in accordance with the schedule.

5.3.3 ANALYSIS

The contractor's progress in conducting and completing the ILS effort described in the Statement of Work and meeting System Specifications will be measured through review of deliverables and progress against schedule and budget at the various reviews. Monitoring of cost, schedule, performance and technical milestones, critical path analyses and overall program status will provide checks and balances to ensure program supportability risks in terms of complying with the Supportability Strategy are identified quickly and accurately. The Logistics IPT will analyze the risk in terms of actions and events in the context of WBS elements and specific work packages to determine the impact on cost, schedule, performance and supportability. Identified risks rated as moderate or high will be aggressively managed and will become an agenda at each management or IPT review.

6.0   PROGRAM RISK SUMMARY

Risk management is a key component of the UH-60M Acquisition Strategy. The RMP was developed to: 1) summarize the UH-60M risk mitigation activities to date and those that are planned for subsequent program phases, and 2) document how DoD directives have been adapted to develop a process to evaluate risk inherent in Army acquistion programs. The RMP also serves as a guideline to the UH-60M team to ensure a standardized approach to the risk mitigation process is utilized.

The architecture of the process takes advantage of existing organizational structures; contractual data requirements; and meetings/reviews of informational exchange to develop a disciplined process to identify, assess, document, and continuously update program risk elements. The UH-60M risk management process is a careful assessment of technical concerns and requires the IPT membership's judgement to define the effort required to reach practical solution. The event-driven nature of this approach, whether through technical, cost, schedule, or supportability information channels, ensures that all milestones demonstrate achievement of a practical, producible, and supportable engineering design that meets the user's requirements.

6.1   RMP UPDATES

The risk management process is a disciplined management technique that is applied to a dynamic, ever-changing acquisition process. Therefore, the process must not only provide an initial identification and assessment of risk elements, it must also be applied continuously as a pro-active process to gain and maintain control over risk elements. Consequently, an RMP update process will be keyed either by Milestone events or by PM-directed periodic reviews. At such time, a thorough review will be conducted and updates made as necessary.

6.2   INTEGRATED RISK ASSESSMENT

The IRA compiles risk assessments from technical, cost, schedule, and supportability functional areas. The IRA will be used in support of the Milestone decisions. The initial IRA is provided in support of MS I/II and will be updated prior to MS III. The initial IRA provides the latest risk assessment and the baseline for the UH-60M program risk activity.

Index

About the Author

 **E** lisabeth Wright is a member of the full time faculty of the School of International Graduate Studies at the US Naval Postgraduate School in Monterey, CA. She is also the Program Manager for the International Defense Acquisition Resources Management program at the school. Prior to her appointment, she served on the faculty of the University of Mary Washington and as the Director of the Master of Science Program in Acquisition Management at the George Washington University, School of Business and Public Management. Professor Wright holds her doctorate from the University of Southern California, School of Policy, Planning and Development and additional degrees from Florida Tech and the University of Maryland. Prior to her career in academia, she was a senior level acquisition manager within the Department of the Navy and the Department of Energy. Professor Wright is designated a Certified Professional Contracts Manager (CPCM) and was awarded the distinction of Fellow by the National Contract Management Association. She has authored numerous articles on procurement and contracting and is an internationally recognized expert in the field.

Other books published by
NIGP: The Institute for Public Procurement

INTRODUCTION TO PUBLIC PROCUREMENT

THE LEGAL ASPECTS OF PUBLIC PROCUREMENT

DEVELOPING AND MANAGING REQUESTS FOR PROPOSALS IN THE PUBLIC SECTOR

CONTRACT ADMINISTRATION IN THE PUBLIC SECTOR

SOURCING IN THE PUBLIC SECTOR

STRATEGIC PROCUREMENT PLANNING IN THE PUBLIC SECTOR

ALTERNATIVE DISPUTE RESOLUTION

FUNDAMENTALS OF LEADERSHIP AND MANAGEMENT IN PUBLIC PROCUREMENT

LOGISTICS AND TRANSPORTATION

CAPITAL ACQUISITIONS

CONTRACTING FOR PUBLIC SECTOR SERVICES

CONTRACTING FOR CONSTRUCTION SERVICES

WAREHOUSING AND INVENTORY CONTROL

NOTES: